The Great War

Great Aycliffe, Brafferton and Coatham Mundeville Remember

Published by Aycliffe Village Local History Society

© Aycliffe Village Local History Society 2014

The men and women in this book are related to people now living in the

Great Aycliffe, Brafferton and Coatham Mundeville area.

Produced and Edited by Vivien Ellis, B.A. Hons., M. Litt.

Acknowledgements

Many thanks to the hard work and help from Harry and Audrey Moses, David and Elizabeth Lewis, Vivien and David Ellis, David Baker, David Blair, June Palmer, Denis Dryden, John Osborn, Ken and Pam Fox, John and Joyce Malcolm, all the relatives of those remembered and members of Aycliffe Village Local History Society who provided photographs and information.

Also many thanks to all staff and pupils of Greenfield Community College and Aycliffe Village Primary School and the support of Chris Lloyd of The Northern Echo.

Also the Commonwealth War Graves Commission who provided information and gave permission to use their material.

This book would have been impossible without the grant from the Heritage Lottery Fund, for which we are extremely grateful.

AYCLIFFE MEMORIAL.

Contents

Students' work from Aycliffe Village Primary School and Greenfield Community College, Newton Aycliffe, has been placed at intervals from pages 22 - 144.

FOREWORD

The First World War was declared on the 4th August 1914. The British Expeditionary Force (BEF) comprising four infantry divisions and one cavalry division arrived in France on the 14th August, shortly joined by two more infantry divisions. These were highly trained, well disciplined soldiers with considerable skill in arms. On the 23rd August they clashed with the advancing German forces on the Mons Canal in Belgium. Although heavily outnumbered, the British infantry, with its renowned rapidity of rifle fire, inflicted heavy losses on the Germans but were forced to retire under the increasing pressure. At Le Cateau, on the 26th August, II Corps turned and fought a rearguard action in an attempt to slow down the enemy advance, which gained valuable time to enable the rest of the BEF to retire more or less unmolested. In October and November the First Battle of Ypres was fought. By the end of the year the original BEF comprising some 100,000 regular soldiers suffered such losses as to cease to be a force capable of holding its own with the German Army. The war was not over by Christmas 1914 and, until the final victory and armistice in November 1918, over three quarters of a million men serving with our forces were killed. Many more suffered physical wounds, and severe mental and emotional traumas, which never left them throughout their lives. So many were unable to talk of their ordeals and others could only do so in old age.

Mons, Le Cateau and First Ypres were the first of many battles that the British Army would fight over the next four and a quarter years. During this period our Colonial forces, particularly from the Indian Continent, along with volunteers from Canada, Australia and New Zealand made up the British Army. Shortly after the outbreak of war, Lord Kitchener made his famous appeal, 'Your Country Needs You' and volunteers flocked forward to join 'the war that would be over by Christmas'. We know that it was to last much longer. Territorial battalions volunteered to serve abroad in October 1914 and took their place in the Army. In 1916, following heavy losses and the volunteer element drying up, conscription was introduced by the Government. The major battles fought throughout the war involving the British Army are listed in the following pages.

Aycliffe Village Local History Society, when considering what it could do in this centenary year of the beginning of the conflict, decided to apply for a Heritage Lottery Grant, which was successful and the Society was awarded £10,000 enabling it to purchase essential equipment and meet the cost of publishing a memorial book recording as many forebears of people living in the Great Aycliffe Area, Brafferton and Coatham Mundeville. We have been able to do this with the considerable assistance and support we have had from the local community, members of which have trusted us with their family records. The members of the families who served in World War I are listed in the following pages, together with whatever information was given to us and more which we have been able to discover from other sources. We are grateful to the families who have contributed to it.

The book could never have been produced without the efforts of a small, hard-working committee. Vivien Ellis, ably supported by her husband David and David Lewis, has been at the very centre of our operation, receiving the information, searching records and producing the final book. The other members of the committee have carried out research tasks and have done all that they were asked to do in support. All have given of their time and effort. The result speaks for itself as the book is a unique record of over two hundred men and four ladies who served our country during this desperate conflict. It is a moving record and one which will appeal to those seeking family histories, military and social researchers. It will, I am sure be an important addition to the history of our village and surrounding area.

Harry Moses, B. Ed. (Hons)

Chairperson,

Aycliffe Village Local History Society,

September 2014.

Aycliffe Village War Memorial

COATES, Anthony. b. 1887 in Monks End, Aycliffe.

1891 census: Parents shown as Hannah, née Coates, and Michael McCormack of Monks End, Aycliffe. His father is employed as a Drainer and came from Ireland.

1911 census: Anthony is listed under the surname McCormack, 23 years old, single and employed as a drainer. The family was still living in Aycliffe and consisted of four sons and four daughters.

Army number: 3889. Rank: Lance Corporal.

Unit: 5th Battalion, Durham Light Infantry.

Enlisted: Darlington (Orleans, Aycliffe).

Killed in Action: September 15, 1916, the first day of the Battle of Flers-Courcelette on the ridge between Bazentin-le-Petit and High Wood.

Buried: Adanac Military Cemetery, Miraumont, north of Pozières.

Anthony is commemorated on the War Memorial, St. Andrew's Church, Aycliffe.

Hannah McCormack,
Anthony's mother

DUNN, Alexander George. b. March 6, 1894 in Middridge, Co. Durham.

Parents: William Dunn and Ann Oliver.

Family: eleven siblings.

1901 census: at Eden Pit, Middridge. The eighth child was Alexander G. Dunn, age 7.

1911 census: the family had moved to Woodham North Farm. Alexander was at Trimdon Grange, age 17, working as a farm servant for John Davison.

Alexander died April 7, 1921 and was buried in St. Andrew's Churchyard, Aycliffe April 11, 1921 and is commemorated on the War Memorial.

Unit: unknown.

DUNN, Oliver Edward. b. November 28, 1895 in Middridge. Brother of Alexander above.

1911 census: Oliver is working at Windlestone Farm as a general servant for Joseph Hughf.

Army number: 201685. Rank: Private. Unit: 4th Battalion, Yorkshire Regiment.

Killed in Action April 23, 1917.

Oliver's name is on the Arras Memorial at Faubourg, Bay 5.

EADE, Aylmer. b. 1892 in Aycliffe Vicarage.

Parents: Reverend Charles John Aylmer and Constance Eade.

Family: two siblings, John and Charles.

1901 census: Aylmer was a boarder at school in Spondon, Derbyshire.

1911 census: at home with parents in Aycliffe Vicarage.

Rank: 2nd Lieutenant. Unit: 3rd Battalion, Yorkshire Regiment.

Killed in Action: died of wounds received at Poelcapelle, October 9, 1917, age 25.

Buried: Cement House Cemetery, Langemark-Poelkapelle, north of Ypres, West-V., Belgium.

Grave Ref. VII. E. 7.

Aylmer is commemorated on the War Memorial, St. Andrew's Church, Aycliffe.

EADE, Charles. b. 1891 in Aycliffe Vicarage. Elder brother of Aylmer above.

Rank: Lieutenant. Unit: 9 Machine Gun Corps.

GELL, Charles Frederick. b. 1883 in Stillington.

Parents: Richard and Eliza Gell.

Family: wife Annie Elizabeth, née Roberts, married 1902, and six children: Eva, born 1902, Lily, born 1904, Charles Frederick, born 1911, Helena Elizabeth, born 1915 and twins, Florence Miriam and Mary Alice, born 1919, 6 months after their father was killed.

1911 census: living in the High Street, Aycliffe. Charles was a bricklayer.

Army number: 87504. Rank: Private. Unit: 13th Battalion, Kings (Liverpool) Regiment.

Charles enlisted at Darlington. He was first Sapper 179002, Royal Engineers.

Killed in Action: September 1, 1918.

Buried: Ecoust-St. Mein British Cemetery, north east of Bapaume, Pas de Calais, France.
Grave Ref. A. 37.

Charles is commemorated on the War Memorial, St. Andrew's Church, Aycliffe.

GOUNDRY, Henry. b. 1896 in Bolam, Co. Durham.

Parents: John and Julia Goundry.

Family: four brothers, two sisters.

1901 census: Henry is entered as Harry, age 6.

1911 census: family living at Woodham Farm, Ferry Hill.

Army number: 32141. Rank: Private.

Unit: 2nd Battalion, Durham Light Infantry.

Enlisted: December 10, 1915. He was 19 years 5 months old, 5' 5" in height and weighed 134 lbs. Henry was approved as fit for general service and first joined the 4th DLI.

Henry was at Seaham from May 3, 1916 to August 2, 1916 and then joined the Expeditionary Force September 1, 1916 as part of the 2nd Durham Light Infantry.

Killed in Action: Henry was reported wounded and missing October 15, 1916.

Henry was not married and had no children. On the Statement of Relatives sheet in his records, Henry's father was dead. His mother, Julia Jane, lived at 3, Cleveland Street, Cockton Hill, Bishop Auckland. His brother, John Oliver, was 32, at Woodham Farm, Rushyford, Frederick William, 30, at Woodham South Farm, Ralph Stanley, 21, at Cockton Hill, Frank, 19, Percy, 17, at Cope Law, Woodham, Aycliffe. His sisters were Cicely Mary Kendall, 25, at High Head, Aycliffe, and Norah Jane Pearce, 23, at Middridge House.

Henry's grandparents were dead. His nephews and nieces were Gertrude Mary Kendall, 4, of Aycliffe, Elizabeth Ellen Goundry, 2, and John Goundry 1½, Annie Stephenson Pearce, 10 months. His aunts and uncles were Thomas John Wyld of Bishop Auckland and William Watson Wyld of Australia.

Henry is commemorated at Thiepval, Pier and Face 14A and 15C.

Henry is also commemorated on the War Memorial, St. Andrew's Church, Aycliffe.

Henry's sister Cicely Mary had married Robert Kendall in 1914. Cicely and Robert Kendall are the grandparents of Mrs Hodge of Darlington, who has kindly provided the photographs of Henry and Robert.

MATSON, Alfred. Baptized March 25, 1893 in Aycliffe.

Parents: Thomas and Mary Matson of Tanyard Cottages, Travellers Rest.

Family: brother of Charles below, William, age 34, of 18, Wilson Street, Hopetown, Darlington and his sister Olive Kent, 32, of 1, West House, Aycliffe, wife of Frederick Joseph Kent.

Army number: 143200. Rank: Gunner.

Unit: D Battery, 107 Brigade, Royal Field Artillery.

Killed in Action: July 17, 1917, age 23.

Buried: Lijssenthoek Military Cemetery, Poperinge, West-Vlaanderen, Belgium,

Grave Ref. XVI. D.

Pte. Charlie Matson, 18th D.L.I. (Puls.), brother of Mrs. F. Kent, Aycliffe.

MATSON, Charles. Baptized November 10, 1896 in Aycliffe.

Army number: 18/113. Rank: Corporal.

Unit: 18th Durham Light Infantry.

Attested: September 5, 1914 at Darlington in the 18th DLI, Special C Batt. DLI.

Charles was 19 years old. He was an apprentice boilersmith at Robert Stephenson Company.

Charles was not married. He was 5' 7" tall, weighed 133 lbs and his chest measured 34 inches. His complexion was fresh, eyes brown and hair brown.

Charles embarked in England December 6, 1915 and disembarked at Egypt December 25, 1915. March 5, 1916 he embarked at Egypt and disembarked at France March 11.

Charles was wounded July27/8, 1916. He was back with his unit in the field August, 26 1916. He was promoted to Corporal December 1, 1916.

The 95th Field Ambulance (France) reported March 2, 1917, that Charles had died age 21 from his wounds received in action March 2, 1917.

August 1917 Thomas Matson wrote to acknowledge receiving his son's effects - coin, letters, photos, pipe, testament, wallet, pouch, cig. case, A.F.D. 455H., but noting that 4 articles were missing, and a notebook that he had in his possession when home last October is not the same as the one sent. He hoped this matter would be looked into.

Charles is buried at Sailly-au-Bois, north west of Beaumont-Hamel, Grave ll.A.12.

Charles and Alfred are both commemorated on the War Memorial, St. Andrew's Church, Aycliffe.

PRATT, Edward Henry. b. 1889 in Cockerton.

Parents: Nicholas Joseph Pratt of Scorton and Jane Anne Fletcher.

Family: married Margaret Louisa Watson, 1908 in Darlington. He had four children.

1911 census: living in Heighington Street, Aycliffe.

Army number: 201248. Rank: Private.

Unit: 5th Battalion, Durham Light Infantry.

Attested October 25, 1915. Edward was living at 15, I'Anson Street, Darlington. Edward was 26 years 10 months old. He was 5' 6" tall and had good vision and physical development.

Edward joined the Expeditionary Force in France February 10, 1916 and received a gun shot wound (mild) to his left leg and to his neck. He was home for 3 months and then went back to France June 15, 1916. He received a gunshot wound to his right shoulder September 16, 1916.

Edward was home September 25, 1916 to March 21, 1917 and then returned to France. He was in France March 22 to November 1917. By May 21, 1918 he was discharged as being no longer physically fit for war service. He had scars on his chest, back, left arm and wrist.

Edward was 29 years 6 months old, 5' 8" tall, had a ruddy complexion, blue eyes, and light brown hair. His address at this time had been Well Bank, Aycliffe, but on one discharge form it is given as Horlines (Orlands now), Aycliffe. Edward's Medical Report April 20, 1918 states that his disability was cerebral injury, optic atrophy, partial paralysis left side. Edward had been buried in a dug out, this causing the cerebral injury.

Edward's children on his Disablement Pension Award Sheet are John Nicholas, born March 21, 1911, Sidney, born September 27, 1913, and Marjorie Jane, born September 9, 1916. Alfred E, who was in the 1911 census, is not mentioned.

Tuesday, September 17, 1918 The Northern Echo had the following notice in the Roll of Honour: "PRATT,- At Greenbank Hospital, Darlington, September 15th, Pte. E. Pratt, D.L.I., died from wounds, aged 30 years, the beloved husband of Margaret Pratt, of Aycliffe. Interment at West Cemetery on Thursday, leaving Cockerton at 9.15. Friends please accept this (the only) intimation."

> PRATT.—At Greenbank Hospital, Darlington, on September 15th, Pte. E. Pratt, D.L.I., died from wounds, aged 30 years, the beloved husband of Margaret Pratt, of Aycliffe. Interment at West Cemetery on Thursday, leaving Cockerton at 2.15. Friends please accept this (the only) intimation.

Kind permission of The Northern Echo

In the records for West Cemetery for September 19, Edward Henry Pratt, 29 years, died (Greenbank) Hospital, (of Orlands, Aycliffe). Buried by the Rev. W. A. Dickinson, Registrar Joseph Bowker. Edward is buried in an unmarked grave, Section Q, Row 7 H, Plot 138.

Edward's wife died October 22, 1922, age 33, and is buried in St. Andrew's Churchyard, Aycliffe.

Edward Henry Pratt is the grandfather of Stephen Gibson and Margaret Prest of Darlington, who has now placed a grave marker on Edward's grave.

Margaret Prest and Aycliffe Village Local History Society are seeking a headstone from the Commonwealth War Graves Commission for Edward.

ROBINSON, Joseph. Baptized December 5, 1897 in Aycliffe.

Parents: Anthony and Sarah Elizabeth Robinson.

1911 census: family living in the High Street, Aycliffe.

Army number: 203113. Rank: Private. Unit: 1/6th Durham Light Infantry.

Killed in Action: May 30, 1918. His name is on the Soissons Memorial. Soissons is east of Compiègne.

Joseph is commemorated on the War Memorial, St. Andrew's Church, Aycliffe.

Alan Pattison says that his grandfather, James Parker, married Elizabeth Robinson, sister of Joseph, in 1915.

ROBINSON, Walter. b. 1887 in Aycliffe.

Parents: George and Sarah Robinson of North Row, Aycliffe.

Family: wife Catherine Young. Brother of Arthur, Fred and Benjamin below.

Army number: 203818. Rank: Lance Corporal. Unit: 20th Battalion, Durham Light Infantry.

1901 census: family living in Orlans in Aycliffe. Walter was still at school. In the 1911 census Walter was still single, living as a boarder at 4, Dale Street, Chilton. He was a Miner Hewer. Walter's parents and family were now living in North Row, Aycliffe.

Killed in Action: September 21, 1917, age 30. Commemorated: Tyne Cot Memorial, Belgium, Panel 128 to 131 and 162 and 162A.

ROBINSON.—In affectionate and loving remembrance of Lance-Corpl. Walter Robinson, 203818, 20 Durham Light Infantry, aged 30 years, killed in action September 21, 1917, the dearly-beloved husband of Catherine Young Robinson, 6, King's Street, Gateshead, and the dearly-beloved son of George and Sarah Robinson, of Aycliffe, Darlington.

Why was he taken so young and so fair,
When the world had so many it better could spare;
Hard, hard was the blow that compelled us to part
With one so near and dear to our hearts.
In the springtime of life, with its joys just unfolding,
From our midst he suddenly fled;
It went to our hearts like the cold blast of winter,
As the whisper went round he was dead.
When alone in our sorrows and bitter tears flow,
There stealeth a dream of the sweet long ago,
But unknown to the world you stand by our sides,
As whisper these words, "Don't fret, death cannot divide."

Ever remembered by his loving wife, father, and mother, his loving sister Daisy, brothers, Ben in France, Arthur and Fred, prisoners of war in Germany.

With kind permission of the Evening Despatch, Saturday, 21 September 1918, the following Roll of Honour In Memoriam notice appeared on the first anniversary of Walter's death.

Walter is also commemorated on the War Memorial, St. Andrew's Church, Aycliffe.

ROBINSON, Arthur, M.M. and Bar. b. 1892 Aycliffe.

Army number: 19/86. Unit: 22nd Battalion, Durham Light Infantry.

Arthur won the Military Medal And Bar. The Military Medal award was printed in the Northern Star, September 20, 1917. Prisoner of War in Germany.

ROBINSON, Frederick. b. 1898 Aycliffe.

Army number: 7105. Rank: Private. Unit: 9th Battalion, Durham Light Infantry. Prison of War in Germany.

ROBINSON, Benjamin. b. 1900 Aycliffe.

Army number: 23022. Rank: Private. Unit: 52 Nottingham and Derbyshire Regiment.

SCOTT, William Rutherford. b. 1892 in Aycliffe.

Parents: George and Mary Scott of Monks End, Aycliffe.

Family: husband of Margaret from Coatham Mundeville, brother of Charles below.

Army number: 22/738. Rank: Lance Corporal.

Unit: 22nd Battalion, Durham Light Infantry.

Killed in Action May 27, 1918, age 26.

Commemorated: Soissons Memorial, east of Compiègne and on the War Memorial, St. Andrew's Church, Aycliffe.

The photograph appeared in The Northern Star, November 7, 1916.

Pte. W. R. Scott, Aycliffe.

SCOTT, Charles Rutherford. b. October 8, 1893 in Aycliffe.

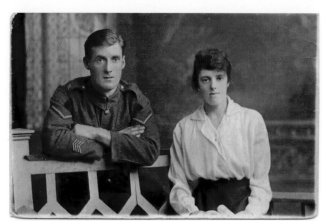

He married Ada Stabler in 1918 and had a son, William, born 1919, and Muriel, born 1921.

Rank: Lance Corporal.

Unit: Royal Engineers.

Charles died July 22, 1945.

Charles Rutherford Scott and Ada Stabler

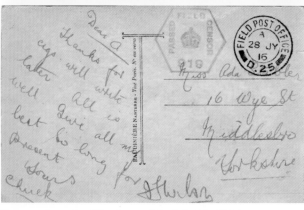

Postcard sent by Charles to Ada July 28, 1916

Charles and Ada Scott are the parents of Muriel Scott of Aycliffe. Muriel herself worked in a munitions factory in WWII.

SLATER, George Alfred. b. 1900 in Darlington.

Parents: Robert Thomas and Margaret Slater of East Ville, Aycliffe.

Family: brother of Charles Henry, Robert Corney, John James, Thomas William and Emma Slater.

Army number: TR5/160067. Rank: Private.

Unit: 53rd Northumberland Fusiliers.

Died of wounds: June 29, 1918 at Cannock Chase Military Hospital, Rugeley Camp, Staffordshire.

Buried: July 3, 1918, St. Andrew's Churchyard, Aycliffe.

George is commemorated on the War Memorial, St. Andrew's Church, Aycliffe.

With kind permission of the Evening Despatch, the Roll of Honour death notice appeared on Monday, July 1, 1918 and on the next two days. Also the funeral was reported as being the first military funeral that had taken place in the village.

Private G. A. Slater, Northumberland Fusiliers, was interred with military honours on Wednesday, at Aycliffe, this being the first military funeral that has taken place in the village.

ROLL OF HONOUR.

SLATER.—Died at Cannock Chase Military Hospital, Rugeley Camp, Staffordshire. Pte. G. A. Slater, youngest son of R. T. Slater and the late Margaret Slater, of East Ville, Aycliffe, Darlington, aged 18 years. Interred at Aycliffe this (Wednesday) afternoon. Friends please accept this (two only) intimation.

WARDLE, Edward.

Edward's name is on the War Memorial at St. Andrew's Church, Aycliffe. Nothing is known about him. Is he related to the Wardles below?

WARDLE, John Alfred. b. 1880 in Evenwood, Co. Durham.

Parents: Edward and Mary Elizabeth Wardle of Cockfield.

Family: married Martha Anderson 1914. Residence: Tan Yard Cottages, Aycliffe.

Army number: 3914. Rank: Private. Unit: 1st/6th Battalion, Durham Light Infantry.

1901 census: at Blue House, Lands, Evenwood, is the family of Edward and Mary Elizabeth Wardle (née Wilson) with their 6 children. John Alfred was the 4th child, age 21, a Coal Miner Hewer.

1911 census: Edward Wardle had died and his wife Mary was living at Lands Bank, Cockfield with her son William, and 2 grandsons, Fred and Herbert, sons of her daughter Elizabeth.

Killed in Action: October 1, 1916, age 35.

Commemorated: Thiepval Memorial, Somme, France, Pier and Face 14 A and 15 C.

WARDLE, Herbert, M.M. b. 1896 in Evenwood.

Army number: 131539. Rank: Sapper.

Unit: 234th Field Company, Royal Engineers.

Attested: August 12, 1915.

Family: Grandson of Edward and Mary Wardle, nephew of John above.

Herbert was awarded the Military Medal March 23, 1916.

Killed in Action: July 31, 1917. Herbert is buried in the New Irish Farm Cemetery near Ypres, Grave Reference XIV.F.7.

His grandmother received his medals.

Brafferton WW1 Memorial Plaque

Originally in

Mary Magdeline Church

Coatham Mundeville

BARTON, John. b. 1881 in Sunniside, Co. Durham.

Residence: Willington, Co. Durham.

Parents: Ralph and Margaret Barton.

Family: Four brothers and one sister. Wife Elizabeth, son Aubrey, and daughter Mary.

Army number: 11216, then 50879. Rank: Private.

Unit: Royal Fusiliers, then C Company, 8th Battalion, Royals Fusiliers, City of London.

1901 census: John is an Elementary School Teacher, living at South Bank, Normanby.

John then moved to teach at Brafferton School.

November 11, 1915 William is travelling on the White Star Line ship "Adriatic" from New York to Liverpool. He is a teacher. His address is 2, Rosedale Terrace, Willington, Co. Durham. With John were his wife Elizabeth and son Aubrey R, age 9 and daughter Mary J, age 2.

Killed in action November 2, 1916, age 35.

Commemorated at Dainville Communal Cemetery, western outskirts of Arras.

Grave Reference: A.7.

John is also commemorated on the bronze Memorial Plaque now in Brafferton Village Hall.

HAWKSLEY, John Plunkett Verney, D.S.O. b. 1878 in Tenby, Pembrokeshire.

Parents: James Taylor Hawksley and Emily Julia, of Caldy Island, Pembrokeshire.

1891 census: John was a scholar.

Rank: Lieutenant Colonel. Unit: Royal Field Artillery.

John Hawksley joined the army and served in the South African and Sudan Campaigns (South Kordofan, 1910). John rose to become Lieutenant Colonel of the Royal Field Artillery. He lived at Thorpe Place, Chertsey, Surrey.

John had received the Order of Osmanieh (4th Class) and the D. S. O., and was mentioned three times in despatches.

Killed in Action: August 8, 1916, age 38.

Commemorated at Becourt Military Cemetery, Becordel - Becourt, south east of Albert, Grave Reference: I.V.28.

John is also commemorated on the bronze Memorial Plaque now in Brafferton Village Hall.

John's elder sister, Muriel Emily, married Robert Bradley Summerson of Hall Garth, Coatham Mundeville. Muriel applied for her brother's 1914 Star.

MARQUIS, Archibald Scott. b. 1885 in Hamsterley, Co. Durham.

Parents: William Marquis, born Morley, Co. Durham and Dinah Scott, born Tow Law.

1891 census: family were at Morley.

1901 census: at High Moor Farm, Hamsterley. Living at the next farm, Low Moor Farm, was Thomas Marquis and his family. Presumably Thomas and William were brothers.

1911 census: family at Dene Head. Archibald has yet to been found in the 1901 and 1911 census.

Army number: 32567. Rank: Private. Unit: 2nd Battalion, Durham Light Infantry.

Killed in Action: June 21, 1917, age 31. Commemorated: Maroc British Cemetery, Grenay, north west of Lens, Grave II.D.8.

Archibald is also commemorated on the bronze War Memorial Plaque at Brafferton Village Hall.

Archibald had married Edith Hannah Vickers of Aycliffe in 1916. Edith is probably a cousin of William Vickers, who was killed in 1918. She is in the 1891 census at Stanley Farm, next to New House Farm, and was there in 1901 when William Vickers was at New House Farm.

Archibald's brother John Scott Marquis married Sarah J Robinson and had a son named Archibald March 24, 1922.

Archibald's brother William Cowling Marquis married Minnie Ellwood in 1921. His daughter is Hilda Nixon of Aycliffe, who kindly gave the photograph of Archibald.

MARQUIS, David Cecil. b. 1891 in Morley, Co. Durham. Brother of Archibald above.

Army number: 34/143310. Rank: Sergeant. Unit: 20th Field Battery, Royal Army Service Corps.

Attested: October 11, 1915 at Bishop Auckland. He was 24 years 9 months old and was a butcher, living at Coatham Mundeville. He was 5'8" tall and weighed 134 lbs. He joined the Army Service Corps Supply Branch, 5/4/143310.

David was tested in the A.S.C. Butchery October 13, 1915, and proved himself a fair butcher, but hadn't yet been tested in slaughtering. David was posted October 12, 1915, appointed Lance Corporal November 17, 1915, and Acting Sergeant January 28, 1916.

David embarked at Southampton February 17, 1917 and disembarked at Le Havre February 21, 1917 from SS Huntscraft. He joined the 20th Field Butchery March 20, 1917.

David was transferred to U.K. for release Group 1 February 25, 1919.

PEIRSON, Taylor. b. 1889 in Darlington.

Parents: John Peirson and Elizabeth Mary Hodgson.

1911 census: Taylor is single, living with his parents and three of his five siblings. They lived at 82, Westmorland Street, Darlington. Taylor's father was a railway engine driver, and Taylor himself worked as a railway clerk.

Family: married Margaret Bamlett in October, 1913.

Army number: 21426. Rank: Sergeant. Unit: 12th Battalion, Yorkshire Regiment.

Killed in Action: died of his wounds April 10, 1918, age 28.

Taylor is remembered in the Haverskerque British Cemetery, north west of Béthune, Grave A.6.

Taylor is also commemorated on the bronze War Memorial Plaque at Brafferton Village Hall.

SLATER, Charles Henry. b. 1895 in Darlington.

Parents: Robert Thomas and Margaret Ann Slater.

Family: four brothers including George Alfred, who is commemorated on the War Memorial at St. Andrew's Church, Aycliffe, and one sister.

1901 census: family at Harrogate Hill, Darlington.

1911 census: living with his parents and siblings at 37, Longfield Terrace, Honeypot Lane, Harrogate Hill, Darlington.

Army number: 17784. Rank: Lance Corporal.

Unit: 9th Battalion, Alexandra, Princess of Wales's Own (Yorkshire Regiment).

Enlisted in Darlington.

Killed in Action: June 7, 1917.

Commemorated: Menin Gate, Ypres, Panel 34.

Charles is also commemorated on the bronze War Memorial Plaque at Brafferton Village Hall.

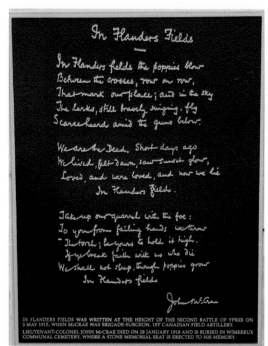

John McCrae's poem

"In Flanders Fields"

at the

Advanced Dressing Station, Essex Farm, north of Ypres

TWEDDLE, John. b. 1888 in Coatham Mundeville.

Parents: Thomas Tweddle and Elizabeth Ann Biglin, both born Coatham Mundeville. They had had nine children, two of whom had died by the 1911 census. Thomas Tweddle was a machine riveter.

Army number: 12227. Rank: Lance Corporal. Unit: 8th Battalion, Border Regiment.

Killed in Action: April 28, 1916.

Commemorated in La Chaudière Military Cemetery, Vimy, Grave VII.D.7.

John is also commemorated on the bronze War Memorial Plaque at Brafferton Village Hall.

VICKERS, William. b. 1893 in Coatham Mundeville.

Parents: Charles Henry Vickers and Mary Jane Robinson of New House Farm, Coatham Mundeville.

1901 census: there are four sons, including William. At the next farm, Stanley Farm, is John Vickers with a brother and two sisters. Are these Charles's siblings?

1911 census: Charles Henry Vickers was a widower with three sons and one daughter living with him at New House Farm, Coatham Mundeville.

William emigrated to Australia aboard the Armadale, departing October 28, 1913 at London and arriving at Fremantle. He must have returned home as he is on the Orsova, departing January 15, 1915, bound for Australia. He lived at Kalgoorie, Western Australia (gold prospecting?). He was 23 when he arrived in Australia.

Army number: 2242. Rank: Corporal. Unit: 32nd Battalion, Australian Infantry.

He enlisted into the Australian Infantry in 1915.

Killed in action March 16, 1918.

Commemorated on the Menin Gate, Ypres, Panel 7-17-23-25-27-29-31.

William is also commemorated on the bronze War Memorial Plaque at Brafferton Village Hall.

Great Aycliffe

Timeline 1914

June 28: Archduke Franz Ferdinand assassinated in Sarajevo.

August 1: Germany declares war on Russia.

August 3: Germany declares war on France and begins invasion of Belgium.

August 4: Great Britain declares war on Germany.

August 23: B.E.F. in major conflict at Mons, Belgium.

October 30: 1st Battle of Ypres, Belgium, begins.

December 16: Hartlepool, Whitby & Scarborough shelled by German Fleet.

December 25: Christmas Truce on parts of the front line. Football match between British and German troops in No Man's Land.

Courtesy of Lewis Atkinson

ATKINSON, John. b. 1892 in Darlington.

Parents: John Thomas and Sarah Jane Atkinson.

Family: married Elizabeth Simpson Wanless 1918.

Unit: 20th Battalion, Durham Light Infantry.

John was wounded and as a recently discharged wounded soldier, he got involved with the Darlington Branch of the Discharged Sailors and Soldiers Association (DSSA.).

January 13, 1918 he was elected a Branch Committee member, (Northern Despatch 14/1/1918).

1919 John moved to Aycliffe, where his son John was baptized August 15, 1920.

Also in 1919 he was a founder member of the Association's Branch at Aycliffe, being appointed Secretary (Northern Echo 15/4/1919). The DSSA was a forerunner of the British Legion.

John Atkinson served in The Observer Corps in WW2, second left in the photograph above.

John is the father of The Reverend Canon Lewis Atkinson.

AVERY, Alfred Edward. b. 1896 in Stockton, Co. Durham.

Parents: John Thomas and Dorothy Avery.

1911 census: the family were living in Brunswick Street, Darlington. Alfred had 2 brothers and a widowed elder sister.

Army number: 47143. Rank: Private. Unit: 5th Machine Gun Corps (Cavalry).

Attested: September 3, 1914. He first served in the 13th Royal Regiment of Cavalry, no. 20566, then the 2nd Royal Regiment of Cavalry, no. 20099 and finally in the 5th Machine Gun Corps (Cavalry).

Alfred received his Protection Certificate of Identity January 26, 1919, at which time his address for pay was 3, Melville Street, Darlington.

On his Certificate of Employment During The War it states that Alfred had been a bricklayer before enlisting. He is described as a good hardworking man, conscientious and reliable and who has done very good work with his unit throughout. He was very good with horses. His military qualification was 1st Class M. Gunner (V).

During WW1 Alfred was gassed and it affected him afterwards, probably contributing to his death from pneumonia March 17, 1929.

Alfred Edward Avery is the grandfather of Dennis Avery of Aycliffe.

Sharing in The Trenches

Sharing the bad

Sharing the good

Sharing diseases, the cold, the wet

Sharing parcels, food and fags

The worst thing of all is sharing the pain

Which slowly changes into sharing death

Hannah Tarn, aged 10

Aycliffe Village Primary School

BAKER, George William.

b. 1897 in Skipwith, Yorkshire.

Residence: York.

Parents: George William and Ann Baker.

Family: One brother and two sisters.

Army number: 312280. Rank: Gunner.

Unit: Royal Garrison Artillery, 269 Siege Battery.

Attested: Tower Street Armoury, York in 1914.

George served at Blyth Shore Battery, and at Ypres in 1915. He also served in Egypt and Mesopotamia - along the Tigris to Baghdad.

George served after the war in India at the Governor's Residence in Simla (Shimla).

Photograph courtesy of David Baker

George returned home on the P&O RMS Kaiser-I-Hind (an Indian wind) to Plymouth in 1919.

In WW2 George served as a sergeant in the Home Guard at York.

Medals: 1914 -1918 Victory Medal and the 1939 -1945 Defence Medal.

George is the father of David Baker of Aycliffe.

BELL, Henry James. b. September 11, 1885 in New Shildon, Co. Durham.

Parents: James Bell and Elizabeth Robson.

1891 & 1901census: family now at Willington. Henry's father was a coke drawer, while Henry was a labourer at the brickworks.

Henry served in the army prior to WW1 but the regiment is unknown.

Rank: Signaller. Unit: East Surrey Regiment.

Henry was wounded and captured early 1916 and remained a prisoner of war until the end of the war.

Henry is the maternal grandfather of Keith Bell of Newton Aycliffe.

BIRCHALL, Thomas. b. September 6, 1888 in Market Drayton, Shropshire.

Parents: Thomas and Annie Birchall. Thomas Birchall senior, a printer, died less than a month later, December 10, 1888.

1911 census: Thomas, his mother Annie and brother William were living at 55, Shrewsbury Road, Market Drayton. Thomas was a liveryman for the Ginger Beer Works.

Army number: 14/294. Rank: Sergeant.

Unit: 14th Battalion, York and Lancaster Regiment.

Courtesy of Ken Fox

Killed in action: July 1, 1916. Commemorated: Thiepval Memorial, Pier and Face 14A & 14B.

Thomas had moved to the Barnsley area and worked as a miner. Thomas had also served in the 4th Kings Shropshire Light Infantry as a territorial soldier.

Thomas enlisted January 22, 1915. His address was Greta Terrace, Shafton, Barnsley. He joined the 14th Battalion, 2nd Barnsley Regiment which became known as The Barnsley Pals.

July 1, 1916, 0740 hours, B company, under Major Guest, followed A company into No Mans Land. Leaving Rolland trench Thomas Birchall made his way towards the German lines. He had not advanced far when he was struck by machine gun bullets from the German Maxim 08 and died where he fell.

Thomas Birchall is the great uncle of Ken Fox of Aycliffe.

Thiepval Memorial

*Photograph courtesy of
David Blair*

BLAIR, John. b. July 23, 1883 at 35, Telford Street, North Ormesby.

Parents: William Blair and Isabella Trewhitt.

Wife: John Blair, age 27, married Mary Brown, age 24. He was a Boilerman.

August 5, 1903, John joined the Royal Navy, initially for 5 years.

Rank: Stoker 2nd class. Ships: Pembroke, Anson, Leandy (Myrridon) and the Kent.

John served for a time in the British Asiatic Squadron, and was part of the visit made by the Royal Navy to Tokyo in July 1906.

August 1908, John had served his initial period of service and moved into the Royal Fleet Reserves, as Stoker 1st Class and annually kept his drill days and competency, as well as a regular bounty.

July 12, 1914, John was recalled to the Navy and joined HMS Goliath for training and moved from there to the Pembroke. By September 17 he was in the 2nd Royal Naval Brigade, then the Victory IV Hood Battalion, Leading Stoker SS100012.

During the War John saw active service both in Belgium and in the Dardanelles.

John Blair is the grandfather of David Blair of Aycliffe. David gave the information and photographs.

John Blair's medals

BLENKINSOPP, Joseph. b. 1896 in Aycliffe. Residence: High Street, Aycliffe.

Parents: Robert and Thomasina Blenkinsopp. Both father and son were butchers.

Family: Nine brothers and sisters.

Army number: 90189. Rank: Bombardier. Unit: 51 Royal Field Artillery.

Joseph attested August 27, 1914. He was 19 years, 147 days old. He was 5' 8 ¼" tall, weighed 144 lbs and had a 37" chest. He had blue eyes and fair hair. Joseph was a railway porter at this time.

Dates of his postings are hard to read. May 11, 1915 he embarked at Southampton and arrived at Le Havre the next day. He had leave to the UK December 19-29, 1916.

October 19, 1917 he was appointed A/Bombr, vice "George" died of wounds. Joseph was admitted as wounded this day and then re-joined from hospital October 25, 1917.

February 9, he had influenza, returning to duty March 16, when he then embarked for UK on posting to Dispersal Centre for Demobilization.

BLENKINSOPP, Jack. b. 1900 in Aycliffe. He was the brother of Joseph above.

Unit: unknown.

BLOOMFIELD, Edward. b. 1883 in Wigan, Lancashire.

Parents: Robert Bloomfield and Ellen Molyneux.

1911 census: the family were living at 157, Staffordshire Street, Sacriston, Co. Durham. Edward was staying with an aunt and uncle, Mary Ann and William Thirlaway, at 2, East View, Station Town, Wingate, Co. Durham. He was working as a coal miner hewer.

Edward married Eliza Dover September 16, 1911.

Attested: February 27, 1915 at Durham. Edward was 32 years 2 months old. He was 5' 1" tall.

Army number: 19/122. Rank: Private. Unit: 19th Battalion, Durham Light Infantry.

Edward embarked for France from Southampton January 31, 1916. He was transferred to the 173rd Tunnelling Company, Royal Engineers, March 20, 1916 and served in the field.

July 13, 1916 he was then attached to the 1/6th West Yorks Regiment. A week later Edward received a gunshot wound to his head. He was sent back to England August 8, 1916.

Edward was posted to the 14th Battalion, Durham Light Infantry April 1917. June 11, 1917 he disembarked at Boulogne.

Edward was killed in action November 20, 1917 at the Battle of Cambrai, age 34.

Edward is commemorated on the Cambrai Memorial, Louverval, Panel 10.

Edward Bloomfield is the great uncle of Marian Galloway of Newton Aycliffe.

BODDINGTON, Thomas.
b.1880 in Carlton, Durham.

Parents: Joseph and Margaret Boddington.

1881 census: parents and three children were at Cape House Farm, Redmarshall. Tom was 9 months old.

Army number: 419002.

Rank: Lance Corporal.

Unit: Labour Company, West Yorkshire Regiment.

1911 census: Tom and his sisters Jane and Lizzie were running the Gretna Green at Travellers Rest.

Tom married Isabella Boddy, sister of Joseph and William Boddy, in 1914.

They had two daughters, Hilda, born 1915 and Ida, born 1920.

Ida married Thomas Hadrick and

Hilda married John Lax.

Tom Boddington later lived at 1, Tannery Cottages, Travellers Rest and died May 13, 1940.

Photographs courtesy of
Mrs Ida Hadrick.

War

The cause I am fighting for never stops
Neither do the lice or the rats eating the dead.

As artillery shells fly
My comrades die.
I begin to wish I was home instead.

It was meant to be an adventure - a story to tell
It ended up being an earthly hell.

Cameron Jennings, aged 11

Aycliffe Village Primary School

BODDY, Joseph. b. June 19, 1876 at Woodham, twin of Thompson.

Parents: Thompson Boddy and Jane Ann Bell.

Father's occupation: butcher and owner of the "Hammer and Pincers" (Blacksmiths Arms) at Preston le Skerne.

1911 census: father as Master Butcher, with Joseph, single, a butcher and still living at home. There are three sons and three daughters in the family.

Army number: 67365. Rank: Private.

Unit: Durham Light Infantry and then 162 Royal Defence Corps.

Joseph married Elizabeth Mary Longstaff in 1917. Their son John Robert Boddy was baptized September 7, 1919.

Photographs courtesy Mrs Ida Hadrick, niece of Joseph and William

BODDY, William Anthony.

b. December 27, 1889 at Woodham,

Brother of Joseph above.

In the 1911 census William was 22, working as an assistant butcher for his father.

Unit: 15th Battalion, Durham Light Infantry.

A medal card for a William Boddy has been found: Private 39202, Durham Light Infantry. He received the Victory and British War Medals.

In a newspaper article in the Darlington & Stockton Times, August 15, 1959, William's life is reported in an article about the Hammer & Pincers. William was 70 and the third generation to hold the licence of the old beer house. His father Thompson had taken over in 1880 and William himself in 1933. William spent most of his life there, apart from his service with the 15th Battalion, Durham Light Infantry and a few years at the Redworth Arms.

William bought the Hammer & Pincers in 1947 and made it a free house.

William married Hannah Elizabeth Giggeson of Middridge in 1926.

William died 1968, and 2 years later his son Jim sold the Hammer & Pincers.

Joseph and William Boddy are the brothers of Isabella Boddy who married Thomas Boddington.

Photograph courtesy of
Joyce Malcolm

BOWERBANK, Robert. b. May 22, 1892 in Coxhoe, Co. Durham.

Parents: Robert and Margaret Bowerbank.

Enlisted: November 23, 1914. Robert was 22 years 6 months old. He was 5' 6 ½" tall. His next of kin was his wife Alice, née Huggins, and he had 5 children, Nora, Joseph, Edith, Maria Ellen, and Mary Ann. Maria lived in Newton Aycliffe for over 40 years.

Army number: 16697. Rank: Private.
Unit: 6th Battalion, Yorkshire Regiment (Green Howards).

Robert served in Gallipoli and then was posted to France July 2, 1916. He received a gunshot wound which led to his discharge January 3, 1917.

December 27, 1917 Robert received his War Badge and Certificate. The Badge was to be worn on the right breast or on the right lapel of the jacket, but not in Naval or Military uniform.

Robert Bowerbank is the grandfather of Joyce Malcolm, née Bowerbank, of Newton Aycliffe.

A War Wish

I march along helmet on my head

Wishing I was still at home in bed.

Sunset comes

Darkness falls.

Back into the trenches I go

Hiding away from my foe.

I'm not with my family

I'm with the rats instead.

Still wishing and praying

I was back at home in my bed.

Ellsa and Alana, aged 11

Aycliffe Village Primary School

BOWMER, George. b. June, 1887 in Bonsall, Derbyshire.

Parents: George and Matilda Bowmer.

1911 census: George is with his brother Harry and Harry's family at The Mills, Great Longstone, near Bakewell, Derbyshire. George and Harry are cotton doublers in the cotton mill.

Attested: November 4, 1914 at Bakewell.

Army number: 3488. Rank: Private. Unit: 6th Battalion, Sherwood Foresters.

George was 27 years, 5 months old. He was 5' 4" tall, weighed 121 lbs, had a pale complexion and had brown eyes and dark brown hair.

George was discharged December 4, 1914 as medically unfit for war service.

BOWMER, Francis. b. 1890 in Bonsall. He is the brother of George above.

Attested: November 12, 1914 at Buxton.

Army number: D 27910. Rank: Private. Unit: Army Service Corps.

Francis was 24 years 4 months old, was 5' 5 ½" tall, weighed 133 lbs, had a fair complexion and had brown eyes and hair.

Francis served 118 days until he was discharged as medically unfit March 9, 1915.

BOWMER, Thomas. b. 1895 in Bonsall. He is brother of George and Francis above.

1911 census: Thomas is working as a butcher's boy.

Attested: November 29, 1915 at Bakewell. He was living at Slaley, Bonsall and was a gardener. Thomas was 20 years and 262 days old. He was 5' 11" tall and weighed 153 lbs.

Army number: 31969, then 63195. Rank: Private.

Unit: 19th Battalion Nottingham and Derby Regiment (Sherwood Foresters), then 7th Battalion, Royal Defence Corps.

July 3, 1916 Thomas joined the British Expeditionary Force and was transferred to the 11th Battalion, Sherwood Foresters July 12, 1916. The Sherwood Forester took part in the 3rd Battle of Ypres July 31, 1917. Thomas was then transferred to the 7th Battalion, Royal Defence Corps September 1, 1917.

Thomas was discharged October 12, 1917 with the disability of ankylosis of the left elbow.

Thomas and Francis Bowmer are mentioned in a WW1 poem "The Bonsall Lads".

George, Francis and Thomas Bowmer are great uncles of Ian Bowmer of Aycliffe.

BRANNIGAN, John. b. 1872 in Consett, Co. Durham.

Army number: 8/4070. Rank: Private.

Unit: 1st/8th Battalion, Durham Light Infantry.

John died December 27, 1916 and is commemorated at St. Sever Cemetery Extension, Rouen.

John Brannigan is the maternal grandfather of Edmund Leadbitter of Aycliffe.

A soldier's life in war

In the trenches

Little food to share

Lots of illness and death

Lice in my hair

Rats sleep with me

Some the size of cats

I awake to them

Nibbling, nibbling at my flesh.

On the battlefield

Muddy boots weigh me down

Bodies all around

Crying, shooting, banging sound

Pain and blood

Then peace

I feel and hear no more.

Adam Dixon-Dawson, aged 10

Aycliffe Village Primary School

BRIGGS, George. b. 1884 in Leasingthorne, Co. Durham.

Parents: James Briggs and Mary Dunn.

George married Annie Trusdale September 1, 1909.

1911 census: George and Annie and their baby Doreen Hazelhurst Briggs were living in Cornforth Lane, Co. Durham. George was a coalminer stoneman. Sadly Doreen died in 1911 and Annie in 1915, age 30.

Attested: November 9, 1914. George was 30 years 8 months old. He was 5' 9" tall, weighed 144 lbs, had a sallow complexion, blue eyes and dark brown hair.

Army number: 14922, then 100133, then 205869. Rank: Private.

Unit: East Yorkshire Regiment, then Durham Light Infantry and then RAMC.

George was first in the East Yorkshire Regiment, in which he served until January 27, 1917. George had been in France March 15, 1916 till July 8, 1916. He had received a gunshot wound to his right hand and thigh.

George was then transferred to the Durham Light Infantry, Private 100133 April 24, 1918. George remained in England until he was discharged after the war April 26, 1919.

During his war service George had qualified as a 1st Class Signaller.

For some reason George re-enlisted August 28, 1919 into the RAMC, Private 205869, under a false name - Joe Watson. His occupation was grocer. His next of kin is given as Mrs Emma Young, Lumley View, Newfield, Newcastle on Tyne. This enlistment was for 1 year.

George Briggs is the great uncle of June Taylor of Newton Aycliffe.

BRUCE, Arthur Robert. b. April 10, 1894 in Brafferton.

Parents: Robert Robinson Bruce, blacksmith, born in Brafferton, and Ann, born in Ripon.

Family: One sister, May Bruce. Arthur married Minnie Lawson in 1915. He had a son, Albert Ronald Robert Bruce, born 1917 and a daughter, Frances Ellen, born 1921.

1901 census: family are at Brafferton and by the 1911 census Arthur was working as a blacksmith's assistant for his father.

Army number: 205 HH. Rank: Gunner. Unit: Royal Artillery.

Attested: June 24, 1916.

Arthur was discharged August 25, 1917 due to illness.

Timeline 1915

April 22: 2nd Battle of Ypres. Germans use poison gas for the first time.

April 25: Start of Gallipoli campaign.

May 1: Lusitania sunk by German U-boat.

May 31: Battle of Jutland, North Sea.

October 5: British and French land in Salonika, Greece.

BUCKLE, Ernest William. b. 1881 in Eryholme, Yorkshire.

Parents: Alfred Buckle and Isabell Wake.

1901 census: family living at Heighington. Alfred Buckle was a farmer and butcher, while Ernest was still at school.

1911 census: Ernest was a boarder at 2, Dixon Terrace, Darlington. He was working for N.E.R. as an Engineer Mechanical Iron Planer. He was 22 years old.

Army number: 4406, then 34997. Rank: Colour Sergeant.

Unit: Durham Light Infantry, then Yorkshire Light Infantry.

Ernest married Isabella Simpson Matson in 1916. Their son Alfred William was baptized 1919.

Isabella was the daughter of William Matson, and Mary Ann Robinson (the daughter of Jarvis Robinson).

The Matson family were living at Heworth Cottage, Aycliffe in 1911. William Matson was a foreman drainer working for himself. His son, **William Jervis Matson,** also served in World War 1, unit unknown.

Beaumont-Hamel

BUCKTON, Mary Jane & SHAW, Hannah.

Found in the Evening Despatch for Saturday, July 21, 1917 is a photograph of two women, both from Aycliffe.

Miss M, Buckton, grand-daughter of Mr. and Mrs. John Buckton, the first woman to work at Rise Carr ironworks, and Miss H. Shaw, great-grand-daughter of Sir William Chaytor, of Barnard Castle. Both belong to Aycliffe.

Kind permission of The Evening Despatch

Miss M. Buckton is described as the first woman to work at Rise Carr Ironworks.

Mary Buckton was baptized December 22, 1894 at St. Andrew's Church, Aycliffe. Her mother was Betsy Buckton.

1911 census: Mary Jane Buckton, granddaughter, age 16, living with her grandparents John and Mary Buckton, born in Aycliffe.

Mary married William Robinson in 1921 and had a daughter Nancy in 1922.

Hannah Shaw was born 1900 in Aycliffe.

Parents: Alfred Shaw and Hannah Elizabeth Lockey. Alfred was a platelayer, living at Heighington Street, Aycliffe in 1911.

Hannah married Albert John William Outhwaite July 31, 1920.

Whether this is the H. Shaw, great granddaughter of Sir William Chaytor mentioned in the newspaper article is not certain. In the 1881 census there is a Sir William Chaytor, Inspector of Factories, Baronet, J.P., at Croft Hall, Yorkshire.

SHAW, Robert. b. 1894 in Aycliffe. Elder brother of Hannah Shaw above.

Army number: 46323. Rank: Sapper. Unit: Cable Section, Royal Engineers.

BULLEN, George William. b. 1892 at Morton Grange, Durham.

Parents: Benjamin Bullen and Margaret Fuller.

1911 census: the family were living at 13, South Crescent, Fencehouses, Durham. George was working as a coal miner putter.

Army number: 19407. Rank: Private. Unit: Durham Light Infantry.

Attested: September 11, 1915.

BULLEN, John. b. 1891 at Morton Grange, Durham.

John (Jack) also joined the Durham Light Infantry like his brother above.

George and John are the brothers of June Palmer's mother-in-law.

BUNTING, Alfred. b. 1882 in Newbold, Derbyshire.

Alfred's father was William Bunting. Alfred married Sarah Ann Clay December 26, 1904.

1911 census: Alfred, Sarah and their 2 year old daughter Dora were living at 53, Derby Road, Birdholme. There were 2 more sons, Alfred and Edwin, born after the census.

Attested: September 10, 1914.

Alfred was 34 years 147 days old. He worked as a collier. Alfred was 5' 9 ¾" tall, and weighed 142 lbs. He had a pale complexion and had grey eyes and brown hair.

Army number: 16258. Rank: Sergeant.

Unit: Nottingham and Derbyshire Regiment (Sherwood Foresters).

Alfred went to France August 27, 1915 until November 7, 1917. He was promoted to Sergeant March 23, 1916.

Alfred was discharged February 14, 1918, no longer physically fit for War Service. He was 37 years 315 days old. He had been assessed at the 3rd Northern General Hospital, Sheffield. Alfred had been gassed.

Alfred received his Silver War Badge February 20, 1918, together with the King's Certificate.

Alfred Bunting is the maternal grandfather of George Oakley of Newton Aycliffe.

Greenfield Community College

8L Creative Writing Inspired by World War 1 Boxes Created by Year 8

Please note that most of the 13 pieces are untitled. This is deliberate as they are designed to be listened to and students wanted to avoid any distraction from the spoken words. This is especially important in respect of the opening and closing pieces.

1.

On the 28th June, 1914,
after the death of Ferdinand,
I had nightmares, not dreams.
The church bells rang,
as the guns shot: 'Bang!'

On the 22nd April, 1915,
chlorine gas exploded,
as the men's bodies folded.
It was the first German attack;
It moved the French back.

On the 4th May, 1915,
a year into war,
I couldn't bear it anymore.
I signed up with my friend,
to negotiate an end.

On the 7th May, 1915,
I saw a telegram of the dead
caused by a German submarine.
I felt guilty I wasn't there -
"Why is life so unfair?"

On the 15th September, 1915,
The English tanks entered the war -
We thought the Germans would win no more.
It consecutively caused them damage,
but didn't bring an advantage.

On the 12th January, 1916,
it was my time.
The bullet reached me.
The war wasn't over,
but it was for me…

Aidan Wong and Aidan Robson

BURBIDGE, Louis Ethelbert. b. 1875 in Worton, Wiltshire.

Parents: Charles and Annie Burbidge, both of Worton.

Family: wife Rosa, and daughter, Dorothy Rosa. Louis had married Rosa Elizabeth Clissold June 11, 1898 in Paddington. Dorothy Rosa had been born October 25, 1900. Louis was a milk carrier. Dorothy later married Alick Searle.

1911 census: living in the High Street, Aycliffe. Louis was a self-employed grocer. Louis's wife Rosa assisted in the shop, while his daughter Dorothy was at school, age 10.

Army number: 414342. Rank: Private. Unit: Army Service Corps (MT).

Louis was called to service August 1, 1918 at Newcastle upon Tyne. He was 43 years 6 months old, a grocer of the High Street, Aycliffe. He was 5' 4" tall and weighed 131 lbs.

Louis was taught to drive heavy lorries and passed his test October 25, 1918 at O.C. Driving School, A.S.C., Hounslow. The next day Louis was admitted to hospital at Osterley Park with influenza and a temperature of 101.f. His temperature chart for 8 days has survived.

Louis was given his Protection Certificate January 10, 1919.

Louis died November 13, 1955.

*ASC badges courtesy
Bill Lowery*

BURNS, James. b. 1887 in Coundon.

Parents: John Burns and Margaret Ann Spensley.

1911 census the family were at 36-37, Collingwood Street, Coundon. James was a bricklayer.

James served in WW1 as did his brother Spensley below.

Unit: unknown.

BURNS, Spensley. b. 1889 in Coundon.

Army number: C1522. Rank: Private. Unit: King's Royal Rifle Corps.

James and Spensley Burns are the grandfather and great uncle of Keith Bailey of Newton Aycliffe.

2

David's Box: The Day I Went Away

It was a Monday in 1914 and I was ready for a perfect day. 'Fishing,' my grandpa said to me, and a fishing day it would be.

We went out at dawn to the nearest harbour and asked "A boat for today, I would ask please,"

"And a boat you will have. For how long?" the boatman asked.

"Just for couple of hours; here is 10 shillings," grandpa explained. We took the boat out down the ramp, then stood in it. Grandpa rowed us out at least as much so you could see the harbour. We set up the rods with care and then gently laid them down in the water.

We caught five fish. I was so happy. We brought them back to my mum and she cooked them for tea. I sat down and grabbed a fish and as I dropped it the ground shook. 'Was it me?' I thought, but it shook again even louder. I started to worry although my mum had said it was just the target practice with mines. I thought again. Quick as a flash Grandpa spotted enemy planes. It was the First World War. I was 16 at the time and I was old enough to be recruited. My mum came up to me and said, "You may not know what to do, but it is your duty to go."

***

I walked up to a desk with large letters saying 'Sign up to save your country'. With courage I and my Grandpa signed up. I was given a suit with a flat cap and told to put it on. All of a sudden I knew I was on a ship next to my Grandpa hoping for hope along this journey. Three days later my Grandpa died and I could not stop crying. In pain I wrote a letter to my mum and told her all about it including the things about Grandpa. A few days later I received a letter back. She told me to still have faith in myself and get through this till the end.

I arrived in France at what they called a 'mud pit'. I was given a gun and told to sit in a curve in the mud, which they called a trench. We all waited for hours until something happened. People were told to invade the enemy trench in no man's land to scout out the area, so we could get a brief idea of where to go. The scouts were back in an hour and they received chocolate, only a little bar but to them it was like the taste of freedom.

I got another letter back from my mum; she was hoping for me to come back because she had heard about the conditions of life in the trenches. She said, "Please come back safe so that we can be a family again."

And that was the last I ever heard from my mother.

Ryan Aitken

Greenfield Community College

BUTTERFIELD, Thomas. b. 1895 in Shildon. Residence: Heighington.

Parents: Jeffrey Butterfield and Margaret Wright.

Family: Two brothers, one sister and one half brother.

Army number: 19416. Rank: Private. Unit: 15th Battalion, Durham Light Infantry, 69 Brigade, 21st Division.

Enlisted: Darlington (Heighington). Total service: 21/09/1914 - 01/07/1916 -1 year 285 days.

Killed in Action: July 1, 1916, the first day of the Battle of the Somme. Age 21.

Commemorated: Thiepval Memorial, Pier and Face 14 A and 15 C.

Medals: 1914-18 Star, British War Medal and Victory Medal.

Thomas's medal roll states that his half brother John H. Wright, of The Hall Farm, School Aycliffe, received his medals at the end of the war. On the Commonwealth War Graves Commission citation his brother William lived at 7, Heighington Street, Aycliffe.

1901 census for Killerby: Jeffrey and Margaret Butterfield, with sons Peter, born Sheraton, William T., born Killerby, and John J., born Killerby, but no Thomas, who would be about 6 years old. Also there was his widowed mother-in- law, Jane Wright, age 77, born in Ireland. There is also John Wright, stepson, age 10, born Brandon, Durham.

By 1911 Jeffrey was living in Etherley Dene, Bishop Auckland. His wife Margaret had died. He had had 7 children, 2 of whom had died. There was another child, Mary Alice Butterfield, age 6, born Denton. There is also a housekeeper, Meggie Pattinson, age 30, born Usher Moor.

Thomas was 19 years, 149 days old when he enlisted September 21, 1914 at Darlington. He was a farm labourer. Thomas was 5'7" tall, weighed 132 lbs, chest 38", and had brown eyes and light brown hair.

Thomas was posted September 21, 1914, and awarded 7 days F.P.2, November 6, 1915. Thomas was reported missing July 1, 1916, the first day of the Battle of the Somme.

Thomas's half brother, John H. Wright was living at The Hall Farm, School Aycliffe, and his father at Killerby. John signed the Army Form W. 5080, dated May 22, 1920. Thomas had 2 full brothers, William Butterfield, age 22, c/o Mr Wise, Preston le Skerne, Joseph Butterfield, age 20, School Aycliffe, Heighington, a half brother John H. Wright, age 30, School Aycliffe, Heighington, a full sister, Mary Butterfield, age 16, Alms Houses, Staindrop, and 2 nieces, Elsie and Gladys Wright, age 8 & 10, of School Aycliffe.

John had written to the Army Record Office December 21, 1916 stating that he had received a notice from them September 21 reporting that his brother was missing. John was seeking further news.

July 12, 1921 there is a War Office form stating that any articles of personal property should be sent to Mr William Butterfield of 35, Southside, Middridge. William received Thomas's 1914-15 Star and Victory Medal September 2, 1921.

Thomas's metal disc and chain were sent to Mrs K. Wright of Railway Cottages, Aycliffe March 2, 1921.

CARRICK, Thomas Hopper. b. 1885 in Evenwood, Co. Durham.

Parents: William and Mary Carrick.

Family: wife Alice Alderson Tyerman, a son, Wilfred, born 1908 and a daughter, Hilda, born 1909.

Thomas worked as a coal miner.

Thomas served in WW1 but his service records have not been found.

Thomas Hopper Carrick is the grandfather of Thomas Cox

Luke Prescott, 8GBV

Greenfield Community College, WW1 Boxes

India Horner, 8GBV

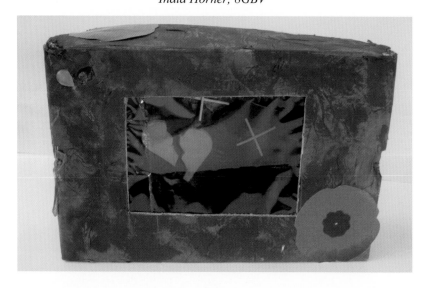

CHRISTIE, Herbert. b. 1890 in Darlington.

Parents: William and Mary Christie of Darlington.

Family: 7 brothers: Married Christine Ibbotson. 2 daughters, Edith and Muriel.

Service number: K/36043. Rank: Stoker 1st class.

Unit: Royal Navy, HMS Opal.

Died: January 12, 1918, Orkneys, age 28.

Commemorated: Portsmouth Naval Memorial, Grave 30.

Herbert Christie is the grandfather of Enid Hugill of Newton Aycliffe.

CHRISTIE, John. b. 1881 in Darlington. Brother of Herbert above.

Family: wife Annie.

Army number: M2/222981. Rank: Private. Unit: Mechanical Transport Reserve Depot (Grove Park), Army Service Corps.

Attested November 28, 1915. He was a motor mechanic and died before he was finally approved.

Died November 28, 1915, age 34.

Commemorated: All Saints Cemetery, Jesmond, Newcastle upon Tyne.

CHRISTIE, Joseph. b. 1881 in Darlington. Twin brother of John.

Family: wife Hannah.

Army Number: 15717. Rank: Private. Unit: 8th Battalion, Yorkshire Regiment.

Killed in Action: June 7, 1917. Commemorated: Menin Gate Memorial, Ypres, Panel 33.

CHRISTIE, William Albert. b. March 10, 1883 in Darlington. Brother of all 3 above.

Family: wife Clara Taylor of Spreydon, Christchurch, New Zealand. Married April 28, 1906, Darlington.

Army number: 64939. Rank: Rifleman. Unit: 2nd Battalion, 3rd New Zealand Rifle Brigade.

Died: July 29, 1918, age 35. Commemorated: Gommecourt Wood New Cemetery, Foncquevillers, north of Beaumont-Hamel, Grave III.D.7.

CLETHERO, Edgar. b. 1896 in Coundon.

Parents: William Clethero of Foulsham, Norfolk, and Susannah of New Shildon, Co. Durham.

1911 census: family at 7, Mill Street, New Shildon. Edgar had two brothers.

Army number: 12094. Rank: Private.
Unit: 10th Battalion, Seaforth Highlanders.

Attested: December 8, 1915 at Darlington. Edgar was 20 years old, of 2, Kilburn Street, New Shildon. Edgar was 5' 6" tall.

Edgar was posted May 23, 1916 to Persia. He served in Egypt January 1918.

October 29, 1918 Edgar was posted to the Royal Engineers as a sapper. October 30, 1918 Edgar was classed as a proficient platelayer, tested on the Military Railways at E.E.F.

Edgar was at Port Said March 8, 1919 and was demobilized April 20, 1919.

Edgar is related by marriage to George Lee of School Aycliffe.

Trenches At Night

Searchlights fill the night sky

Hunting for the aeroplanes as they fly

Then; Bang! Bang! Is what I hear

Bang! Bang! They're very near

Once they have flown away

I lie down in my bed and ask

"What's going to happen in the next treacherous day?"

Hannah Tarn, aged 10

Aycliffe Village Primary School

COLES, Cecil Frederick Gottlieb. b. October 7, 1888 in Kirkcudbright, Scotland.

Parents: Frederick Renius and Margaret Neilson Coles.

Family: he married Phoebe, 1912, and had a daughter Penny.

Cecil was a talented musician, studied at Edinburgh University, and then at London College of Music. He studied with Gustav Holst.

Army number: 390653. Rank: Serjeant Bandmaster.

Unit: 9th Battalion, London Regiment (Queen Victoria's Rifles).

Enlisted: September 2, 1914. Musician and Composer.

Killed: April 26, 1918.

Commemorated: Crouy British Cemetery, Crouy-sur-Somme, Grave I.C.1.

COLES, Herbert Thorwald. b. 1891 in Kirkcudbright. Brother of Cecil above.

1911 census: Herbert Thorwald Coles was serving in the Gordon Highlanders at Colchester. He was a Lance Corporal, age 20. He became CSM.

Herbert Thorwald Coles went to France July 9, 1915.

April 25, 1917 Herbert Thorwald received his commission and served as 2/Lieutenant in the Seaforth Highlanders.

Photographs courtesy Margaret Lee, niece of Cecil and Herbert Coles.

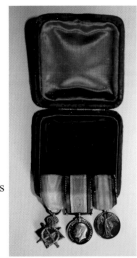

COLES, John Godfrey. b. 1893 in Kirkcudbright. Brother of Cecil and Herbert above.

Army number: 2060. Rank: Private. Unit: Royal Scots.

John entered the war February 24, 1915. John received his commission December 15, 1917. He joined the Gordon Highlanders as 2nd Lieutenant, 292001.

John Godfrey Coles is the father of Margaret Lee of School Aycliffe.

3

Dear Dad,

Hi dad, I know that you are helping our country and I really admire you for that. I hope that you will come home from the trenches to see me and mum soon, as we are both dearly missing you and we are also worried about you.

I understand that you have probably sent us a letter, but because the letters don't get delivered for two to three days - and with the conditions in the trenches - it will most likely be quite hard to read as the water over there has probably made the writing rather blurry. Me and Mam have put you up a little tin with a few small luxuries such as a packet of Woodbine cigarettes and also some chocolate.

I've been reading the magazines. I see that you're doing well but the only thing I do wonder is: whenever you do send letters, some parts don't make sense, as if bits are missing. I've heard stories about how they censor the papers, but that sounds like complete and utter nonsense. Why would they do such a thing?

As you know, I recently turned eighteen and I am now going to try and find a disguise to try and get into the war to come and see you but I am yet to tell Mam about my magnificent plan. I will be telling her soon, but I don't want her to get too worried. You know how worried she was for you - and me being her daughter, she would be even more worried for me. I mean I want to do it, but I just can't bring myself round to causing Mam all that stress.

Money is tight so I will have to find a way to get me and Mam some, but I am not sure how much I can earn and how much my disguise will cost. I'm not even sure if I'll look convincing enough to them because of how I look … now I am getting worried about my sign up. Oh dear!

I want you to wish me luck and all the best and with good fortune, maybe I'll get stationed on the front line and maybe near you!

Yours sincerely

Sarah Laurence x x x

Owen Robinson, Lewis Kilding and Connor Thompson

Greenfield Community College

COULSON, James Hutchinson. b. 1886 at North Aycliffe.

Parents: Jacob and Margaret Coulson.

1891 census: his grandfather, Jacob Coulson, age 74, a widower, was living with the family at North Aycliffe.

1911 census: James was single and working as a farmer along with his father at Aycliffe.

Army number: 168751. Rank: Corporal. Unit: 487 Agricultural Labour Corps.

COX, John Wanless. b. June 21, 1895 in Ramshaw, Co. Durham.

Parents: John Edward and Annie Cox. The family lived in Evenwood, Co. Durham.

1911 census: John was working as an apprentice bricklayer.

Rank: Regimental Sergeant Major. Unit: Highland Light Infantry.

John Wanless Cox is the father of Thomas Cox of Newton Aycliffe.

COX, George Thomas. b. 1888 in Ramshaw, Co. Durham

Brother of John above.

1911 census: George was working as a miner.

Army number: 3472. Rank: Corporal. Unit: 1/6th Battalion, Durham Light Infantry.

Enlisted: Evenwood.

George was killed in action November 5, 1916.

Commemorated: Thiepval Memorial, Pier and Panel 14A and 15C.

Max Hunter, 8GBV

Greenfield Community College, WW1 Boxes

4.

Here I am,

stone cold,

down in the trench.

The fear in the air -

It's too much to bear;

I am lost in my own despair.

My dear wife,

my beautiful daughter,

back home where I long to be.

I see people dying,

Around me they drop.

I wish it would stop.

But it's not long now,

Until I am home

by the fire,

Safe as can be.

But I guess

the only fire I will see

is the burning of buildings

and people turning to dust

right at my very feet!

Rachel Bremner

Greenfield Community College

CREE, Christopher. b. 1878 in Toft Hill, Co. Durham.

Parents: John Henry and Elizabeth Ann Cree.

By 1891 the family had moved to Evenwood.

1911 census: Christopher was married to Elizabeth Ann, with 3 children, Lydia, Laura, and Ronald. He was working as a coal miner in Cockfield.

Army number: 21/1568. Rank: Private.

Unit: 21st Tyneside Scottish, Northumberland Fusiliers.

Christopher died of his wounds February 2, 1916. He is buried at Sailly-sur-la-Lys Canadian Cemetery, Grave II.G.159.

CREE, Adam. b. 1882 in Toft Hill, Co. Durham.

Brother of Christopher above.

1901 census: Adam was working as a coal miner as were his father and brothers.

Adam served in WW1 but his service records have not been found.

CREE, Norris. Brother of Christopher and Adam.

Also served in WW1, service record not found.

Christopher, Adam and Norris Cree are uncles of Thomas Cox of Newton Aycliffe.

Niall Blenkinsopp, 8GBV

Greenfield Community College, WW1 Boxes

5.

Dear Claire,

I'm really missing you whilst I'm out here, like you wouldn't believe. I can't believe it's been a month since I have seen you; it's killing me. By now you will have probably heard the news about Charlie. I won't mention it much because I know he meant the world to you and I am not allowed to talk about the death of fellow troops.

I hope this gets to you because there are rumours around the camp that Germany is bombing the mail boats. However - I know this may sound selfish, but please darling - could you send me some cigarettes and chocolate, if you can get hold of any. I have a massive craving.

I am fine, if you're wondering, and I hope you and Marshall are too. I bet I have missed so much of his childhood … The trenches aren't brilliant, but they're liveable. Its quite cosy: we have high walls made from mud and little bedrooms. We don't get much sleep because we're usually on duty, but we do have good fun. We aren't doing anything much for most of the time. I do things like carving and playing cards. It's all good fun. However the food isn't the best it's probably because I'm used to your lovely cooking. I can't wait to have it again.

In two weeks I should be allowed a leave. I'm in 'The Reserve Trench' at the minute so I'm totally safe. I'm nowhere near the front line.

Writing and receiving messages from you make my day. I love knowing you're safe and writing to you has now become an important part of my routine through the day.

Through the five days it takes for me to receive my letter back from you, I am so apprehensive to hear all your news, good and bad.

Enjoy the souvenirs I have sent you, I hope the buttons come in useful.

With love,

Your Husband

XXXXXXX

Harry Hobbs and Blake Metcalfe

Greenfield Community College

CRUSHER, Joseph Henry. b. 1893 in Middleton St. George.

Parents: Benjamin Crusher and Ada Coulson.

Family: four sons and one daughter.

1901 census: family at Lop Leach Carr, Aycliffe. Benjamin is a farmer.

1911 census: address is just Travellers Rest, Aycliffe. Joseph is not on this census with his parents.

Army number: 127306. Rank: Bombardier. Unit: No. 4 Depot, Royal Garrison Artillery.

Enlisted: Darlington December 11, 1915.

Joseph was called up for service at Ripon November 3, 1916. He was with 13 Company December 18, 1916, and at Anti Aircraft Company January 20, 1917. November 30, 1917 he became Pa/L/Bdr and was appointed Acting Bombardier in the 43rd A.A. Company February 23, 1918.

Joseph was given his Protection Certificate and Certificate of Identity January 4, 1919.

CRUSHER, Robert Barker. b. December 20, 1896 in Aycliffe. He is the brother of Joseph above.

1911 census: Robert is working on the farm for his father. The family were living at Field House, according to the photograph below.

Army number: 163149. Rank: Private.

Unit: 4th Division, Royal Engineers.

Robert died May 20, 1986, age 89 and is buried in St. Andrew's Churchyard, Aycliffe, as is his wife Alice, who died April 23, 1963, age 59.

Driver R B CRUSHER (R.E.), of Field House, Aycliffe.

Photograph: Thursday, 20 July, 1916, with kind permission of the Northern Evening Despatch

CRUSHER, Thomas. b. 1894 in Aycliffe.

Army number: 521268. Rank: Private. Unit: 412 Agricultural Corps. Brother of Joseph and Robert above.

1911 census: Thomas is a horseman at North Farm, Walworth, Darlington.

Timeline 1916

January: Conscription of unmarried men starts in Britain.

February 21: Start of the Battle of Verdun, France.

May: Conscription extended to married men.

June 5: Lord Kitchener dies on HMS Hampshire en route to Russia.

June 26: Bombardment starts on the Somme, France.

July 1: British and Colonial attack starts on the Somme.

September 15: Tanks used for the first time at Flers, France.

November 13: British take Beaumont-Hamel, Somme.

November 18: Battle of Somme ends.

DALE, Robert Addison. b. 1884 in Dinsdale, Co. Durham.

Parents: John Kirby and Anne Dale.

Army number: 7/7097, then 277283. Rank: Private. Unit: 22 Battalion, Durham Light Infantry.

1891 census: Robert was living with his parents at Fish Lock Cottage, Low Dinsdale. There were five siblings.

1901 census: Robert was a stonemason living in lodgings at 12, Esplanade, Scarborough.

Robert married Betsy Gladwin in October, 1907. They had three children: Margaret Mary Stephanie, born 1908, Winifred, born 1911 and Bessie Gladwin Dale, born 1919.

1911 census: Robert and his wife Betsy were living at Station Terrace, Aycliffe. Robert was a fruiterer. He died December 26, 1962, age 79, and his wife March 7, 1972, age 89 and both are buried in St. Andrew's Churchyard, Aycliffe.

Medals: Victory and British Medal.

DAVIES, Peter Williams. b. 1886 in Wrexham, Denbighshire.

Parents: Aaron Valentine Davies and Tamar Williams.

Wife: Mary Ellen Hughes, born 1887 in Whiston, Lancashire.

1911 census: at East Howle, Durham with his wife and 2 daughters, Tamar and Edith. Peter was a coal miner hewer.

Attested: October 24, 1914.

Army number: 13793, then 573709. Rank: Acting Sergeant, then Lance Corporal.

Unit: 8th Battalion, East Yorkshire Regiment, then Labour Corps.

Presumably Peter had become unfit for War Service, as amongst his medals is the Silver War Badge.

Peter was discharged November 14, 1918.

DAVIES, Benjamin Aaron. b. March 13, 1897 in Hindley, Lancashire.

1911 census: the family were in Ferryhill Station.

Army number: 32830. Rank: Driver. Unit: Royal Field Artillery.

Attested: March 6, 1915. Benjamin was 5' 4" tall, weighed 129 lbs, had a sallow complexion, blue eyes, and nut brown hair. He was a miner. He worked at Chilton Colliery, Ferryhill, Co. Durham. Benjamin's father is next of kin, living at 6, Chapel Row, Chilton Lane, Ferryhill.

Benjamin was in France July 10, 1915 to December 24, 1918, 3 years and 166 days. He was demobilized February 4, 1919.

DAVIES, William Henry. b. April 29, 1899 in Hindley, Lancashire.

Brother of Peter and Benjamin above.

William served in the Royal Field Artillery but his service record has not been found. He survived the war.

Peter, Benjamin and William are the great uncles of Joyce Malcolm of Newton Aycliffe.

Photograph courtesy of Joyce Malcolm

DAVISON, George William. b. September 9, 1891 in Blackhill, Co. Durham.

Parents: Thomas and Dorothy Davison. Thomas had died by the 1911 census. George was working as a Metal Breaker at the Blast furnace. The family were living at 9, East Parade, Consett.

Army number: 350213, then 4441967. Rank: Lance Corporal.

Unit: 6th Battalion, Durham Light Infantry.

George was 20 years 2 months old when he joined the Territorial Army November 30, 1911. He was 5' 8" tall, had a fresh complexion, brown eyes and auburn hair. On his Discharge March 10, 1917, he had served 5 years 111 days.

*Photograph courtesy of
Audrey Moses*

George continued with the Durham Light Infantry from July 17, 1920 to August 20, 1921 and June 27, 1922 to June 26, 1926. He had a new number, 4441967.

From the Medical History of 1922 he was 30 years 291 days old. He was a crane driver. He was now 5' 8 ½" tall and weighed 156 lbs. George was married to Margaret Ellen and lived in Consett.

George William Davison is the father of Audrey Moses of Aycliffe and Vivien Law and Rita Swanwick of Newton Aycliffe.

1st July 1916 Memorial, La Boiselle

DENHAM, Matthew. b. March 6, 1885 in Shildon.

Parents: William and Elizabeth Denham.

Family: Matthew married Olive Mary Kent in 1913. He had 2 children, Josephine Kent, born 1913 and Cyril, born 1915.

Matthew lived at 2, West Terrace, Aycliffe. He worked as a signalman for North Eastern Railways.

Army number: 202611. Rank: Private.

Unit: 8th Battalion, Durham Light Infantry.

Attested: December 11, 1915.

Olive, Cyril, Matthew and Jean Denham

Birthday cards sent to his daughter Josephine (Jean)

Matthew ended his army service with the 4th Battalion, Durham Light Infantry and was discharged March 16, 1919. He had suffered a gunshot wound to his left leg and was slightly gassed in 1918, for which he received a pension of 5s. 6d. (27p) per week from March 19, 1919.

Matthew died February 15, 1929 and is buried in St. Andrew's Churchyard, Aycliffe.

Many thanks to Beryl Wilson of Darlington, who has given us access to her grandfather's World War 1 memorabilia and photographs.

DENT, Frederick. b. 1898 in Aycliffe.

Parents: Henry James Dent, born in Staindrop, a farmer, and Dinah Eales, born Coundon.

1911 census: at Low Moor Farm, Aycliffe.

Army number: 83785. Rank: Private. Unit: Northumberland Fusiliers.

DICKINSON, David. b. 1893 in Kirby Stephen, Westmorland.

Parents: James and Margaret Dickinson.

1901 census: family at Union Square, Kirkby Stephen.

1911 census: David, and Joseph Dickinson, (brother?) age 26, born Kirkby Stephen, were boarders at 89, Craddock Street, Bishop Auckland, working as platelayers for the North Eastern Railway Company.

David married Margaret Robinson August 3, 1912 and lived in the Orlands in Aycliffe. He had 2 children, Maude Evaline and Walter Robinson Dickinson.

Attested: December 11, 1915.

Army number: 31469, 1020, 34672, then 66967. Rank: Private.

Unit: 3rd Battalion, Durham Light Infantry, 2/5th Scottish Rifles, 13th Transport Workers Battalion, Bedfords, then the Labour Corps.

David was transferred to the 13th Transport Workers Battalion, Bedfords January 4, 1917as Private 34672. He was finally he was transferred to the Labour Corps October 26, 1918.

Chiara Timms, 8ROY

Greenfield Community College, WW1 Boxes

George Dickinson and Ethel Dean

DICKINSON, George. b. October 23, 1891, in Ashton under Lyne, Lancashire.

Parents: Thomas and Louisa Dickinson of Ashton under Lyne, Lancashire.

George worked as a cotton minder in one of the cotton mills in Ashton under Lyne.

In December 1915 three sons of Thomas and Louisa Dickinson enlisted into the army.

The family were living at 1, Athol Street, Ashton under Lyne.

Frederick and George enlisted into the 9th Battalion, Manchester Regiment and Stanley Dickinson enlisted December 12, 1915 into the Army Service Corps (M T). He was a taxi driver, age 22 years 3 months. Stanley was mobilized February 17, 1916. By May 6, 1918 Stanley was discharged as no longer physically fit for war service. Stanley was 5'5" tall, had a fair complexion, light blue eyes, and had light brown hair.

George Dickinson married Ethel Dean November 16, 1916 at the Albion Congregational Church, Ashton under Lyne.

George Dickinson, Private 351812, now 1/8th Manchester Regiment, was killed August 30, 1918.

His name is on Panel 9 in the Vis en Artois Cemetery near Arras, the War Memorial at Ashton under Lyne and he is remembered on the headstone of Ethel's parents in the churchyard at Leyland, Lancashire.

George Dickinson was the first husband of the grandmother of Vivien Ellis of Newton Aycliffe.

DOVE, Albert William. b. 1893 at Thornley, Co. Durham.

Parents: John Dove and Sarah Armstrong.

1911 census: the family were living at Front Street, Haswell.

Family: wife, Ada, and a child. They lived at 9, Pyman Street, Wheatley Hill.

Enlisted: December 1914 at Sunderland. Albert was by then living at Wheatley Hill. He was a putter in the Harvey Seam at Thornley Colliery. (*p.79 "The Employees and Residents of Thornley, Ludworth and Wheatley Hill, their contribution in the Great War 1914-1918"*)

Army number: 17766. Rank: Private. Unit: 9th Battalion, Yorkshire Regiment.

Albert was killed in action October 6, 1916. He was 23 years old.

Albert is commemorated on the Thiepval Memorial, Pier and Face 3A and 3D.

Albert is the uncle of Freda McGrath (née Dove) of Newton Aycliffe.

Wheatley Hill Memorial

Thiepval Memorial

Photographs courtesy of John and Joyce Malcolm

The Sad Side Of War

Explosions happening all around

Closer and closer, louder they sound.

A photo of family

Clutched in his hand.

Blood and pain

His cries fading

He's near the end.

Thoughts of family flood his mind

He awakens no more.

Soldiers cry and die together.

Paul Blades, aged 11, Aycliffe Village Primary School

DRING, George, M.M. b. May 30, 1896 at Ferryhill, Co. Durham.

Parents: George and Sarah Dring.

Enlisted: November 28, 1914.

Army number: 17691. Rank: Corporal.

Unit: 9th Battalion, Yorkshire Regiment (Green Howards).

George was awarded the Military Medal for bravery in the field at Contalmaison in the Somme area in July 1916. He was awarded a gold watch by the people of Ferryhill to commemorate his award of the Military Medal.

George died of his wounds June 8, 1917 at No. 10 Casualty Clearing Station, near Poperinge, Belgium. He had been wounded in the Battle of Messines Ridge.

George is buried in Lijssenthoek Military Cemetery, Belgium, Grave XII. C. 9A.

George's grave   *Ferryhill War Memorial*   *Mainsforth Colliery War Memorial*

Photographs courtesy of Joyce and John Malcolm

George Dring is a cousin once removed of Joyce Malcolm of Newton Aycliffe.

DUCK, Arthur. b. June 6, 1897 at Thornley, Co. Durham.

Parents: Edward John Duck and Elizabeth Rowe.

1911 census: the family were living at 7, South Street, Thornley.

Army number: 10303. Rank: Private.

Unit: 7th East Surrey Regiment.

Arthur was now living in Chapel Street, Thornley.

Wheatley Hill History Club have Arthur and his brother Edward John in the list of Absent Voters, page 145 of their book *"The Employees and Residents of Thornley, Ludworth and Wheatley Hill: Their Contribution in the Great War"*.

After WW1 Arthur married Matilda Jane Tonkin in 1923 and then emigrated first to Canada in 1923 and then the following year to Pennsylvania to stay with his uncle, William Freeman.

Edward John, Sarah Jane and Arthur Duck and friend. Photograph courtesy of Alan Wilson.

DUCK, Edward John. b. 1893 at Thornley, Co. Durham. He is brother of Arthur above.

Army number: 100431. Rank: Gunner. Unit: Royal Field Artillery.

After WW1 Arthur married Jane E. Smith in 1919 and then emigrated to the USA in 1927, his family following two years later.

Arthur and Edward John Duck are the uncles of Arthur Wilson of Newton Aycliffe, whose mother is Sarah Jane Duck.

French WW1 75 mm gun at Albert, France

EDWARDS, Charles Robert. b. January 11, 1891 in Brandon, Co. Durham.

Father: Charles Edwards, born Bagillt, Wales.

1911 census: Charles was a widower, age 60, with 4 children still living at home, including a married daughter and her husband and son. Charles senior and Bob (Charles Robert) were coal miners. They lived at 13, Hunter's Terrace, Edmondsley, Co. Durham.

Army number: 20/1489. Rank: Acting Corporal.

Unit: 1st Tyneside Scottish, 20th Northumberland Fusiliers.

Enlisted: February 15, 1915 at the Recruiting Office, at 9, Grainger Street, Newcastle. Bob was 5' 10 ½" tall.

Discharged: March 31, 1919.

Bob was a keen goalkeeper, winning his first medal aged 10. He later combined his job as a miner with playing football in local leagues in Durham.

A match report in the Durham Advertiser February 5, 1915 mentions Bob's "splendid goalkeeping" for Sacriston United in the Durham Central League, and also says that "no less than 17 players from Sacriston United have enlisted".

Bob suffered from the effects of a gas attack. He was in Burnley on his return to England and there met and married Maggie Blakely in March 1919.

Bob is the grandfather of Geoffrey Carr of Aycliffe.

Photographs and information courtesy of Geoffrey Carr

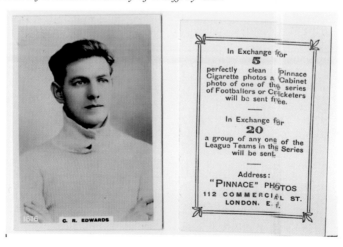

In Exchange for
5
perfectly clean Pinnace Cigarette photos a Cabinet photo of one of the series of Footballers or Cricketers will be sent free.

In Exchange for
20
a group of any one of the League Teams in the Series will be sent.

Address:
"PINNACE" PHOTOS
112 COMMERCIAL ST.
LONDON. E. 1.

C. R. EDWARDS

6

As I sit and stare at the walls of mud,

I think about all the memories I've had,

some good, but many are bad;

Though I'm only a young lad.

I knew straight away as I entered the War Office,

It was going to be the end of me.

And then the letter came.

I felt the pain within me, but

I finally had an aim.

All I have is photos;

That's all they have of me.

I still have the thoughts that one day I'll be free.

The box was my only hope

Of happiness and joy;

I still felt like a little boy

Playing with my toys…

I used to play with toy guns,

but now they are real.

It's the full deal.

My life is a mess,

It's such a stress,

I'm so depressed,

I need a rest!

All I have is my box,

With all the things I have left -

I hope no-ones a thief.

All I can do is dream

about the things that are supreme

and scream the thoughts inside of me.

My life in here is dull.

My medals give me hope

That one day I will be free;

I will see my family once again,

with joy, belief and happy thoughts inside of me.

With all the letters carefully placed,

with love and care from deep within,

It won't be letters soon -

I will be right there

with happiness and care.

There are bullets flying everywhere

all around the air.

I can see the fear in the enemy's eyes.

In dreams I ruled my world:

I'm the hero that spoke these words

"Never give up! Always have hope!"

But now, when I am here in the real world,

I imagine what life would be like,

Away from this awful place.

Shannon Banks, Katie Lovelass and Rachel Lovelass

Greenfield Community College

Inspired by Tom's Box

EVERSON, Frederick. b. May 24, 1887 in North Ormesby, Yorkshire.

Parents: Benjamin Everson and Mary Ann Colley.

1901 census: the family were at 22, Coltman Street, North Ormesby. Frederick was an errand boy for a newsagent.

1911 census: Frederick was a boot repairer, boarding with John and Isabel Knaggs in Chilton, Co. Durham.

December 28, 1914 Frederick married Mary Elizabeth Brown in Middlesbrough. By the time he was embodied they had a daughter Lily, born June 22, 1916.

Attested: December 10, 1915 at Ferryhill.

Army number: 223777, then 306188. Rank: Sapper, then Gunner.

Unit: Royal Engineers, then 13th Battalion, Tank Corps.

Frederick was 28 years 6 months old, 5' 5" tall and weighed 122 lbs. He was a boot maker and repairer. He was living at Tannery Cottages, Travellers Rest, Aycliffe.

January 10, 1917 Frederick had a Trade Proficiency Test at Chatham and was proved Proficient as a Shoemaker.

Frederick served at home until February 23, 1918 when he was sent to France to the Tank Corps.

Frederick was granted leave home October 5, 1918 as sadly his 3 months old daughter Marion had died from convulsions through teething October 2.

Frederick rejoined his unit October 24. January 3, 1919 he returned to England and was demobbed January 17.

Frederick had 2 more daughters, Mary, baptized November 22, 1919, and Freda, baptized October 30, 1921.

Part of the Tank Memorial at Pozières

FAIRNIE, Simon. b. 1880 in Fisherrow, Musselburgh, Midlothian, Scotland.

Parents: Michael Fairnie and Margaret Clark.

Simon was married to Ellen.

Simon served as Skipper 891 WSA, Royal Naval Reserve H.M.S. Trawler "Renarro".

The trawler was sunk by a mine explosion in the Dardanelles, November 10, 1918. Simon was 38 years old.

Simon is commemorated on the Portsmouth Naval Memorial, Panel 30.

Portsmouth Memorial

FAIRNIE, Walter. b. 1888 in Fisherrow, Musselburgh, Midlothian, Scotland. Brother of Simon above.

Walter married Mary Devlin.

Army number: S/2361. Rank: Private. Unit: 8th Battalion, Seaforth Highlanders.

Attested: Musselburgh.

Walter was killed in action September 25, 1915. He is commemorated on the Loos Memorial, Panel 112 - 115.

Walter is the grandfather of Marian Galloway of Newton Aycliffe.

Loos Cemetery

Photographs courtesy Marian Galloway

FARRELL, Michael. b. 1879 in Dublin.

Parents: John and Katherine Farrell.

1901 census: Michael is living with his uncle John Doran in Heighington Street, Aycliffe.

1911 census: Michael had been married to Annie Nelson for 5 years and had 4 children living. They lived at 94, South View, Windlestone. Michael was working as a colliery fireman.

Army number: 3777. Unit: 5th Battalion, Durham Light Infantry.

Attested: July 15, 1915. Michael was 36, 5'8 ¾" tall, in good physical shape and passed fit July 24, 1915. His next of kin was his wife Annie (Nancy) Nelson, and his residence Water Castle, Aycliffe. Michael's children were John born 1904, Kate 1906, Nellie 1908, Richard 1910, Harry 1912 and Mary 1914.

Michael also appears to have been in the Durham Militia 1901 to 1906.

Michael was posted to Blackpool July 1915, then Chelmsford, Essex until April 18, 1917. He then received a new number, 276019, and transferred to the Operating Division, Royal Engineers. He also spent a week at the depot for Railway Troops in Bordon, Hampshire.

Michael was then posted to the Labour Corps at Thetford Camp, Norfolk April 26, 1917. His number was now 207045 and he served in Labour Companies until January 1918. He was then transferred to Agricultural Companies until demobilization in 1919. He received 28 days leave, a £2 advance from his unit 478 Agricultural Company and left from Oswestry February 19, 1919 with instructions for his pay to be sent to 10 Leitrim Drumboyle, Carricon, Shannon, Ireland.

August 1919 there are several signals and demobilization papers to demob Michael out of the 17th Battalion, Yorkshire Regiment, service number 276019.

November 1919 the paperwork still seems outstanding. When Michael claimed his pension on demobilization he added another child, Michael, born 1916. His character was good and he was in B2 medical category.

Michael signed on at the Darlington Employment Exchange in 1919. A letter from Rise Carr Rolling Mills, Darlington, to his Commanding Officer, 487 Agricultural Company in Newcastle offered Michael employment as a Linesman.

Michael went on to have a total of 10 children.

Photograph and information courtesy Kelly Frost, great granddaughter of Michael Farrell.

FARROW, Herbert. b. 1885 in Goxhill, Lincolnshire.

Parents: Isaac and Mary Farrow.

Family: 2 brothers. Married Rosa and had a daughter Rosa and 2 sons, Robert and Ernest in the 1911 census.

Army number: 12/1535. Rank: Private.

Unit: 11th Battalion, East Yorkshire Regiment.

Killed in Action: July 11, 1918, age 34.

Commemorated: Longuenesse (St. Omer) Souvenir Cemetery, Grave V.C.65.

Herbert Farrow is the great uncle of Ronald Kitchman of Newton Aycliffe.

FERGUSON, Thomas Walker. b. 1896 in Hutton Magna, Yorkshire.

Parents: Thomas and Catherine Mary Ferguson. He had 6 siblings.

Wife: Agnes Jane Robinson whom he married December 17, 1938.

Attested: November 17, 1915. Thomas was living at Green House, Gayles, Richmond. He was 19 years 6 months old and was working as a farm labourer.

Army number: 132733. Unit: Royal Field Artillery.

Thomas served in Salonika.

Thomas Walker Ferguson is the uncle of Annette Bowmer of Aycliffe.

FIRBY, Ambrose Binks. b. 1880 in Aycliffe.

Parents: Ambrose Firby and Elizabeth Waistell of Hudswell, Yorkshire.

Wife: Rebecca Light of Aycliffe, married 1903.

Army number: 39673, then 36005. Rank: Private.

Unit: Durham Light Infantry, then 4th King's Own Yorkshire Light Infantry.

1911 census: at 5, Field Street, Darlington. They had had two children, one of whom had died. The surviving child was John Waistell Firby.

Ambrose was captured at some stage in WW1 and became a prisoner of war. He attended the 'Welcome Home Dinner Concert and Dance' for repatriated prisoners of war held at the Temperance Hall, Darlington, May 7, 1919. His address was Brafferton Mill.

Residence: Ambrose lived at Town End Farm, Brafferton where he died August 19, 1958.

Ambrose is the grandfather of Beattie Futter of Brafferton.

FOULGER, George Ernest. b. 1896 in Stockton on Tees.

Parents: George Henry Foulger and Ada Caroline Lawrie, who were living at Filey Road, Stockton on Tees in the 1911 census. George himself was at his uncle Arthur Foulger's home at Esh Winning, Co. Durham. He was a Boiler Maker Helper, age 16.

Army number: 38501. Rank: Private. Unit: B Company, 9th Battalion, Yorkshire Regiment.

George died from his wounds June 13, 1917, age 22.

George is buried in Mendinghem Military Cemetery, Grave II.D.40. This cemetery is 17 kms north east of Ypres.

George Ernest Foulger is the great uncle of Leigh Foulger of Newton Aycliffe.

Photograph may be George Ernest Foulger. Courtesy of Leigh Foulger.

FRANKLIN, Ernest Arthur.

Army number: 201091. Rank: Sergeant. Unit: 1st/4th Battalion, Essex Regiment.

Ernest was killed November 3, 1917.

Ernest is buried in the Gaza War Cemetery, Grave Reference: XXIV. B.7.

Ernest is the maternal grandfather of Margaret Lee of School Aycliffe.

Ernest's medals and death plaque. Courtesy of Margaret Lee.

FURNESS, John Thomas. b. 1879 in Barnard Castle.

Parents: mother Martha Furness.

Family: wife Margaret, née Bell, living at Monks End, Aycliffe, daughter Eva May, born 1906, and a son, John Robert, born 1914.

Army number: 649. Rank: Private. Unit: N.E.R. Battalion, Northumberland Fusiliers.

Attested: September 17, 1914.

John was a platelayer. He was 33 years 4 months old. John was 5' 5 ¾" tall and weighed 140 ½ lbs.

July 5, 1915, John became medically unfit to serve.

John died May 30, 1932, age 54, and is buried in St. Andrew's Churchyard, Aycliffe.

<u>The Trenches</u>

Darkness falls

Soldiers weeping

Soldiers dying

Always loyal

Must keep fighting

Our captain cries out

If he dies

We die with him

I am a soldier

Holding a picture of my child

Will this war never end...

Oliver Hutton, aged 10

Aycliffe Village Primary School

FUTTER, Samuel. b. October 1, 1884 in Merrington.

Parents: Alfred Futter, born in Norfolk, and Mary Ann Gray of Holmside, Durham. They had married in the Stockton area in 1880. In the 1891 census the family were living at Ferryhill and in the 1901 census were at 11, Dixon Street, Blackhill.

Wife: Mary Edith Cherry of Richmond, Yorkshire, whom he married July 19, 1905.

1911 census: Samuel and Mary are living at Leyburn, Yorkshire. Samuel was a limestone quarryman.

Army number: 20238. Rank: Private. Unit: 2nd Battalion, King's Own Royal Lancaster Regiment.

Samuel served as a stretcher bearer. He was later in the Labour Corps, Private 5443/8. He went to France August 3, 1915. The Regiment had been serving at Ypres from May 1915. By September it was involved in the Battle of Loos and by November it had embarked for Egypt, ending up in Salonika January 1916.

FUTTER, Alfred Ascanius. b. January 1892, Ferryhill.

1911 census: at 11, Dixon Street, Blackhill. Alfred was still living with his parents and was working in the Iron Works.

Army number: 158154. Rank: Colour Sergeant: Unit: Durham Light Infantry.

He went to France April 20, 1915.

Alfred married Nora J. Walton in 1919 and had a daughter Audrey.

FUTTER, John George. b. November 26, 1893 at Ferryhill.

John became a sergeant, unit unknown.

FUTTER, Harry Newton. b. September 22, 1899 at Blackhill.

FUTTER BROTHERS. 1914-18 WAR.

Harry served in the Royal Flying Corps as a pilot. He was granted an Honorary Commission as 2nd Lieutenant. This appeared in The London Gazette, April 27, 1920.

Harry married Ellen Taylor Moss in 1922.

Joe and Beattie Futter of Brafferton have given the photographs and information about the four Futter brothers who served in WW1. Samuel is stood left and Harry seated right in the photograph of the four brothers. Samuel is the father of Joe Futter.

GALLOWAY, Walter. b. November 10, 1877 at Cassop, Co. Durham.

Parents: John and Mary Galloway.

Walter was a regular soldier. He had enlisted December 27, 1899 at Newcastle.

Army number: 7012. Rank: Private.

Unit: 2nd Battalion, Durham Light Infantry.

Walter was 5' 3 ½" tall and his physical development was good. He had grey eyes and dark brown hair.

Walter served in the Boer War and was wounded November 20, 1901 at Rietfontein while attached to the 23rd Battalion, Mounted Infantry.

After the Boer War Walter was posted with the 1st Battalion to India and returned to England 1907.

January 30, 1908 Walter joined the First Class Army Reserve. He was recalled to the colours August 1914.

Walter's family received a report January 30, 1915 that he had been killed, but while mourning they received a letter from him dated 2 days after his death.

Sadly Walter died of wounds August 10, 1915 at No. 10 Casualty Clearing Station, near Poperinge, Belgium.

HE IS NOT DEAD AFTER ALL.

Twice Private W. Galloway, of Cassop Colliery, Durham, has been reported as dead when in fact he was alive. The first occasion was during the Boer War. Quite recently his relatives received information that he was killed in action on January 30, but while they were in mourning a letter written two days after his supposed death was received from him.

Walter is buried in Lijssenthoek Military Cemetery, Grave 111, D. 15.

Walter Galloway is the great, great uncle of John Malcolm of Newton Aycliffe.

7

Dear Mum and Dad,

I am writing to tell you that I am scared and frightened that I am going to die in this war and I fear . Today I was scared because my friend was blown up by a hand grenade and his legs were blown off. I am so terrified that I will die in this hellhole and never come home to see you.

I hope I do reach home, so I can be recognised by people as a hero and be able to tell my kids and grandkids the story of how I survived through the fighting – and I hear that the ladies love a soldier. After all, that's why half of us are here in the first place!

All that stuff they said about how we would all join up together – well we were all spilt up into different sections. I don't know anyone here …

Your loving son,

Thomas

Harry Wilson and Kieron O'Connor

Greenfield Community College

8.

It was three o'clock when we awoke;

The gas bell rang as someone choked.

I was scared as it approached me –

it was huge and overpowering.

It destroyed so many soldiers' lives

and also destroyed the soldiers' wives.

The land was distraught: how could it be

That the only person alive – was me?

I couldn't believe what they had done;

They shot the rest down with their guns.

I lay and thought about what I had seen –

why were the enemy so cruel and mean?

We thought that we had lost; we were done,

But then more joined. This won't be fun!

We put our hearts in until we bled,

We fought and fought, but more were dead.

The war was over; the war was done.

I went back home to see my son.

We won the war the English way,

But many of our men had to pay.

The Germans returned to their defeated land;

No one gave them a helping hand.

World War I was England's victory!

But now it is back in history.

Joshua Walker and Joshua Hay

Greenfield Community College

GARTHWAITE, Harry (Henry) Mills. b. June 17, 1894 in Aycliffe.

Parents: Chapman and Catherine Garthwaite.

1911 census: family living at Chapel Square, Aycliffe. Harry was an apprentice mason.

Harry married Eleanor and they had their son, Harry Frederick, baptized December 25, 1920.

Army number: 46318. Rank: Sapper. Unit: 79 Royal Engineers.

GARTHWAITE, Percy John. b.1884 in Aycliffe. Brother of Harry above.

1911 census: Percy was married to Sarah Elizabeth Embleton and was living at 31, Edward Street, Spennymoor. He was a pulleyman working for N.E.R.

Unit: unknown.

GELDARD, Arthur George. b. Coxhoe, Co. Durham.

Arthur served in the Royal Marines in WW1.

Arthur is the grandfather of Mrs Bell of Newton Aycliffe.

GLADWIN, Stephen Victor. b. 1897 in Aycliffe.

Parents: Mary Ann Gladwin, widow.

Family: a sister Margaret.

1911 census: living at Aycliffe House.

Army number: 32943. Rank: Private. Unit: 17th Battalion, Northumberland Fusiliers.

GOLDSBROUGH, Harry Hildreth. b. 1900 in Bowes, Yorkshire.

Parents: William Goldsbrough, a porter, born Barningham, and Annie Isabella.

1901 census: living in Heighington Street, Aycliffe, next door to Henry Nelson and his family.

1911 census: William was still a porter for the N.E.R. He had been married 13 years and had 2 children, but only Harry was at home with them.

Unit: unknown.

Timeline 1917

February 17: Germans start withdrawal to the Hindenburg Line.

March 13: Tsar of Russia abdicates.

April 6: USA enters war.

April 9: British attack Arras.

July 31: Start of 3rd Battle of Ypres - "Passchendaele".

September 20: British gain Menin Road Bridge, Ypres.

November 7: "October" Revolution brings Bolsheviks to power in Russia.

December 9: Allenby captures Jerusalem.

GOODWIN, Charles. b. 1882 in Easton, Norfolk.

Parents: Charles and Sarah Goodwin.

1911 census: Charles was living in Heighington Street, Aycliffe, working as a farm cattle man. He had married Edith Iceton, born in Darlington.

Army number: 250501. Rank: Private. Unit: 6th Battalion, Durham Light Infantry.

Tyne Cot Memorial

69

GOSLING, John Thomas. b. December 4, 1898 in Malta.

Parents: John Thomas Tuxworth Gosling and Mariana Carrillo, who were married August 25, 1894 in Gibraltar.

1911 census: family were living at 24, Tait Street, Carlisle. John had 1 sister and 1 brother. John was still at school.

Army Number: 203167. Rank. Lance Bombardier.

Unit: 397 Battery, Royal Field Artillery, Dundalk.

John was 18 years and 1 month old when he attested. John was a fireman working for the N.E.R.

John was first posted to the No. 2 Reserve Brigade Artillery T.F. January 4, 1917. He was then posted to the 397 Battery, R.F.A Dundalk January 8, 1917. He became a Signaller.

Photograph courtesy of Sue Hindle

John was earmarked for special duty to Belfast January 21, 1919 and was then reposted to R.F.G. Cork May 4 as Pa L/Bdr. British Forces had been used in Ireland since the insurrection in 1916.

John was sent to a Dispersal Centre November 29, 1919.

John Thomas Gosling is the grandfather of Sue Hindle of Aycliffe.

British WW1 gun at Albert, France

GRAINGER, Herbert, M.M. b. October 4, 1891 in Topcliffe, Yorkshire.

Parents: Tom and Jane Grainger. Tom brought his family to Shildon when Herbert was about seven years old in order to have better employment prospects.

1901: family lived at 28, Princes Street, and in 1911 at 13, Princes Street.

1911 census: Herbert Grainger was working at N E R Works at Shildon as a Hammer Driver. Herbert had joined the T. A. in 1908. He served for four years in the RAMC in the 2nd Northumbrian Field Ambulance.

Herbert re-enlisted September 18, 1914 in the 2nd Northumbrian Field Ambulance, RAMC, Private 388209. He was an electric welder, age 22 years 11 months. He was 5 ft 8 ins.

Herbert Grainger was sent to France January 15, 1918 as a stretcher bearer. He served in Ypres, Egypt and Salonika. He suffered from influenza, enteritis and in Salonika became very ill with malaria. He was sent to Malta July 21, 1916 and then to hospital in England October 22, 1916.

Herbert Grainger, sat first left, back row

By August 4, 1917 Herbert Grainger was fit enough to go back to France and embarked at Folkestone. August 6, 1917, he had joined the Cyclist Base at Rouen and was posted to the 11 Stationary Hospital August 11, 1917.

November 1917 Herbert was in the field, and then returned to Rouen. May 1918 he was in the field again, posted back to the 2/2 Northumbrian Field Ambulance. While he was serving in the field Herbert rescued an officer and was awarded the Military Medal. This did not appear in the London Gazette until October 21, 1918.

Herbert Grainger was disembodied April 11, 1919.

Herbert is the grandfather of David Ellis of Newton Aycliffe.

HALL, John William. b. 1894 at Masham, Yorkshire.

Parents: Charles Hall, who was a widower in the 1901 census. Charles and his six children were living at Monks End, Aycliffe. He was working as a mason and bricklayer. They lived next door to Peter Scott, who owned the saw mill. William was still at school.

Army number: 450016. Rank: Private. Unit: 17 Labour Corps.

HALL, Charles Ernest. b. 1896 ay Kirby, Yorkshire. Younger brother of John above.

Army number: 15981. Rank: Private. Unit: 20 K.R. R. G.

Life of a Soldier

In the night

Flares lighting it up the night sky

Searchlights scan the battlefield

Rats nibble at your ears

Wishing you were with your wife and kids.

In the morning

You don't have an ear

The seeping through your skin

Lice crawling all over your body

Dragging your weary body from the trench

On the battlefield

It's Hell on Earth

Dead horses, Dead soldiers

Nothing but death around

The battle you'll never forget.

Oliver Brass, aged 10

Aycliffe Village Primary School

HARDY, John Joseph. b. 1886 in West Hartlepool, Durham.

Parents: Robert and Eliza Hardy.

Family: brothers Thomas and Robert Hardy, wife Frances Elizabeth McNamara.

Army number: 9285. Rank: Private. Unit: The Royal Scots.

John joined the Royal Scots August 3, 1905 at Uphall, Midlothian. He was 19 years 10 months. He was 5' 6" tall, weighed 136 lbs, had a fresh complexion, blue eyes and light brown hair.

John had served in India. In 1913 he was transferred to the Army Reserve. He was then mobilized August 5, 1914. Sadly he became seriously ill and was in hospital at Devonport. There he died two days later, August 7, 1914 and is buried at Plymouth (Western Mill) Cemetery, Grave R.C.C. 11039.

John Joseph Hardy is the uncle of Joe Hardy of School Aycliffe.

HARDY, Robert. b. 1889 in Stockton.

Brother of John above, Robert had joined under age with a false name, but it is not known what that name was. He had joined the 1st Battalion, Durham Light Infantry before the 1911 census and later was in the South Lancashire Regiment.

Robert is the father of Joe Hardy. Joe Hardy himself is one of the last Bevan Boys from WW2.

HARDY, Thomas. b. 1892 in York. Brother of John and Robert above. He served in the war but the unit is not known.

HEWITT, John (Jack). b. 1892 in Coatham Mundeville.

Family: grandson of George and Mary Hewitt.

1901 census: George and his family were at East Row, Aycliffe.

1911 census: living at Orleans, Aycliffe. As well as John Hewitt, there were another two grandsons with them: George Robinson, age 15, a pit labourer, and Fred Robinson, 11, still at school.

Army number: 90206. Rank: Gunner. Unit: Royal Regiment of Artillery.

Attested: August 27, 1914 at Aycliffe. He was 22 years, 269 days old. He was 5' 9 ½" tall and weighed 142 lbs. He had a dark complexion, blue eyes and dark brown hair.

John was posted to the 163rd Battery September 8, 1914. John had been posted to France and was then with the 221st Battery. There was reorganization January 15, 1915 and he was posted to the B Battery, 70th Brigade, RFA, March 13, 1915. When in France John was gas poisoned.

April 14, 1916 John was admitted to the O.C. Sta. Hospital near Salonica, seriously ill and a wire was sent to his father. He was then admitted to the Military Hospital, Valletta April 30, 1916 and his brother was informed.

John was home June 2, 1916 to September 16, 1916, in France September 21, 1916 to December 20, 1917. John returned home December 21, 1917, then was back to France August 10, 1918. He finally returned home March 31, 1920.

August, 1920, John received his 1914-1915 Star Medal and November 5, 1920, he received his British War Medal. In September, 1921 he received his Victory Medal, and was living at 86, High Street, Hemel Hempstead.

Megan Young, 8ROY

Greenfield Community School, WW1 Boxes

HOLLIDAY, George. b. Tuesday, October 13, 1896 in Merrington, Co. Durham. He was 5 minutes younger than his twin brother Thomas.

Parents: Robert and Catherine Holliday.

1901 census: George and Thomas lived with their parents and elder sister Mary Jane.

1911 census: Mary Jane had left home and there were now another 2 brothers John, 9, and Robert, 6.

George and his twin brother Thomas enlisted into the 6th/7th Battalion, Royal Scots Fusiliers. George enlisted October 23, 1915. He was 19, just 10 days after his birthday. He was 5' 4" tall and weighed 118 lbs.

His complexion was fresh and he had blue eyes and brown hair. His regimental number was 20343 and his twin Thomas had the next regimental number 20344.

Tuesday, October 26, 1915 George joined the Royal Scots Fusiliers at Ayr, in Scotland. When he arrived he was posted to the 3rd Battalion. In the early part of 1916 the 3rd Battalion was transferred to Greenock near Glasgow.

George's sister Mary Jane visited George and his brother Thomas in Greenock. They had their photograph taken.

March 14, 1916 George was transferred to the 6th Battalion and embarked for France the next day.

The battalion spent the first 3 months of 1916 in the Ploegsteert section of the front and saw little action.

August 10, 1916 orders were issued for the battalion to attack the German line south of Martinpiuch. George Holliday was one of the 7 casualties in the 6/7th battalion.

George is commemorated on the Thiepval Memorial, Pier and Face 3C.

Photographs courtesy of
Len Skelton

George Holliday is the great uncle of Len Skelton of Newton Aycliffe.

HOLLIDAY, Thomas. b. Tuesday, October 13, 1896 at 4.05 p.m., in Merrington, Co. Durham. He was 5 minutes older than his twin brother George.

Parents: Robert and Catherine Holliday.

1901 census: George and Thomas lived with their parents and elder sister Mary Jane.

1911 census: Mary Jane had left home and there were now 2 brothers John, 9, and Robert, 6.

Both George and his twin brother Thomas enlisted into the 6th/7th Battalion, Royal Scots Fusiliers. Thomas enlisted October 23, 1915. He was 19, just 10 days after his birthday. He was 5' 4" tall.

He had grey eyes and brown hair. His regimental number was 20344 and his twin George had the previous regimental number 20343.

Thomas Holliday. See his brother George's page for the photograph of them together.

October 26, 1915 Thomas joined the Royal Scots Fusiliers at Ayr, in Scotland. When he arrived he was posted to the 3rd Battalion which transferred to Greenock near Glasgow early 1916.

March 14, 1916, Thomas was transferred to the 6th Battalion and embarked for France the next day.

Thomas contracted an infection of the inner ear, otorrhea, and in the field June 16, and July 22 Thomas was treated for an infection of stomach. He was admitted to 12th Stationary Hospital at St Pol, west of Arras till August 3.

April 11, 1917 the 6/7th Battalion attacked the 'Orange Hill' north of Monchy Le Preux. Thomas received a slight gunshot wound in the neck. He was admitted to the 2nd Canadian General Hospital in Le Treport.

Thomas had leave in the UK for a week October 3-10, 1917, then returned to his battalion.

November 1917 the 6/7th Battalion was in the trenches east of Arras. Thomas was badly wounded November 29. A gun-shot entered the abdomen penetrating the right axilla.

A telegram December 1, 1917 informed Thomas' parents that he was 'dangerously wounded with a wound to the abdomen'.

Thomas died of his wounds in the 19th Casualty Clearing Station, France. He is buried at Duisans British Cemetery, Etrun, Grave V. D. 44.

Thomas Holliday is the great uncle of Len Skelton of Newton Aycliffe.

HOLLINGWORTH, Ernest. b. 1890 in York.

Parents: George Hollingworth and Eleanor Thursby, both from Yorkshire.

1911 census: family were living in East Row, Aycliffe. George was a forester, working for the Earl of Eldon, and Ernest a clerk.

Ernest married Margaret Alice Garthwaite in 1914. Their son George Chapman Garthwaite was baptized May 23, 1915.

Army number: 317255. Rank: Private. Unit: Royal Engineers.

Photograph courtesy of Pamela Baul

HORSEMAN, Frederick. b. June 26, 1895.

Army number: 19525. Rank: Private.

Unit: West Yorkshire Regiment.

Attested: April 12, 1915 at Darlington.

Frederick was living at 26, Brighton Road, Darlington, and was 19 years, 9 months. He was 5' 5" tall, weighed 130 lbs and had a chest 37½ inches. His next of kin is listed as Margaret Langthorne, whom he married in 1919.

Frederick was sent to France July 13, 1915.

Frederick was transferred to 2/6th Durham Light Infantry, and then to the Army Service Corps as Private 104160.

Frederick Horseman is the grandfather of Pamela Baul of Newton Aycliffe.

JAGGER, George Alfred. b. 1886 in Leeds, Yorkshire.

Parents: Alfred George Dover Jagger and Maria Jane Speight.

1901 census: George and his brother William were working on East Thickley Farm, Shildon, as a stockfeeder and carter for Elizabeth Weighill.

1911 census: George was living at Heworth Cottage, Heworth House, Aycliffe, with his wife Margaret and daughter Catherine. He was working on the farm. His wife was Margaret Ann White, born Aycliffe, whom he had married in 1909. George had a son, George William, born 1920.

Army number: 201291. Rank: Driver. Unit: Royal Field Artillery.

9

19th October 1914

Dear Daddy,

I'm really missing you and I want you to come home. Mammy is scared and frustrated because we are hiding for dear life, as there are bombs going off all around us. It feels like we are in closed in a dark wall that is keeping us apart. I'm lying in my bed, with my clown, shivering to death, scared about what's going to happen. I am really proud of you dad.

Love Jake xxx

13th November 1914

My Darling,

I am really upset about the sudden departure. I hope you come home soon. I cannot explain the feelings that I experience daily. I hope you come home soon.

Love Anne xxx

19th March 1915

Dear Jake,

We thought it would be done for Christmas.

29th March 1915

Dear Darling,

This Christmas we had roast dinner and little Jake got a war toy and called it   Daddy. We left you a chair during dinner because we thought you were coming home.

Anne

Many letters later….

Brandon Wintour and Joshua Bentley

Greenfield Community College

27th October 1914

Dear Jake,

I'm missing you too son; I cannot wait to come and see you. If you saw what I see now, you would be 'shell shocked'. I think you are a brave little soldier, fighting for freedom, just like me. I hope the Germans back down like the little savages they are so I can come and see you. Do you still love that clown? I bought that for your first birthday.

I will be home before Christmas. I promise. I wrote you a poem:

Shells go off round and round;
My ears now can hear no sound.
As the thunderous Germans charge,
Death and blood are all at large.
And all sanity breaks loose
We will put them in the noose.

Love Dad xxx

25th December 1914

Dear Daddy,

I thought you were coming home today. This Christmas was the worst.

26th March 1915

Dear Daddy,

I am so sorry I did not realise this hope you get home as soon as possible.

1st January 1917

Dear Jake,

I encountered a German today and took a shot to the knee, so I will be coming home early. Whilst I was on leave I got some French candy for you. I hope you are keeping safe. I will be on the boat home, so I will not be able receive letters from you.

Love, Daddy xxx

JESSOP, Lawrence. b. April 1893 in Hillsborough, Sheffield.

Army Number: 822. Rank: Private. Unit: 2nd Northern Company Non Combatant Corps.

Parents: William and Charlotte Jessop.

Wife: Winnifred Pittuck.

Lawrence Jessop was a Baptist and felt unable to serve as a soldier and declared that he was a conscientious objector.

Lawrence was enrolled at Pontefract, May 2, 1916, his enrolment paper stating 'Holds Certificate for Non Combatant Service'.

May 2 - 28 Lawrence was stationed in Richmond, Yorkshire. He was posted to France May 29, 1916 and landed in Le Havre on May 31. He served as a stretcher bearer.

Lawrence was allowed leave was to the United Kingdom, October 1-15, 1918. During this leave he married Winnifred Pittuck, sister of John Pearce Pittuck, Sue Skelton's grandfather.

The war had been over for a year and Lawrence's service was nearly complete.

November 11, at Boulogne, he boarded troop transport 'Maid of Orleans'. At 9.35 a.m. the ship arrived at the Admiralty Dock, Dover.

As the soldiers were preparing to disembark, Private Elliot of the Highland Light Infantry noticed that the bolt of a fellow soldier's rifle, Private William Hood, was open. As trained, Private Hood closed the bolt, pointed the rifle upwards, and pulled the trigger. A shot went off and the bullet passed through the roof to the deck above.

Lawrence Jessop was standing directly above Private Hood on the 3rd lower deck.

The bullet went through his left big toe, grazed his shin, wounded his 2nd finger left hand and passed into his chest. He died instantaneously. RAMC doctor Captain Smith confirmed Lawrence was dead.

The army sent a 'regret to inform you' telegram to his wife Winnifred that afternoon telling her of his accidental death.

A coroner's inquest was quickly held the next day where there was a verdict of accidental death.

The body of Lawrence Jessop was forwarded by rail to Sheffield, November 13, at the request of next of kin. Lawrence's mother lived in Sheffield. His wife Winnifred lived near Benson, Oxfordshire. As next of kin she must have made the decision that his remains would be sent to his family home.

All personal effects were sent to his wife.

Lawrence Jessop must have been one of the last casualties to gunfire of the Great War. He is buried in Wadsley Churchyard, north of Sheffield, Grave 23. EE 44.

Lawrence Jessop is the great uncle of Sue Skelton of Newton Aycliffe.

JOHNSON, Alfred. b. September 3, 1896 at Coxhoe, Co. Durham.

Parents: Edward Johnson and Gertrude Hutchinson. In the 1911 census the family were living at 67, Long Row, Coxhoe.

Attested: January 26, 1914 in the Royal Field Artillery, Gunner 75629. Alfred was 18 years old. He was 5' 6" tall, had a sallow complexion, grey eyes and brown hair.

July 18, 1914 Alfred was discharged from the army.

Alfred then enlisted in the Royal Navy, Stoker 7891S.

He left West Hartlepool June 21, 1915. He arrived at Gibraltar December 28, 1915, then again April 1, 1916. He served on HMS Sappho July 31, 1916 till December 10, 1916. He then served on HMS Biarritz from December 31, 1916 till March 19, 1919 when he was demobilized.

Alfred Johnson is the grandfather of John Malcolm of Newton Aycliffe.

JOHNSON, Joseph Edwin. b. July 22, 1894, Coxhoe, Co. Durham. Brother of Alfred above.

Army number: 83474, then G15415. Rank: Private.

Unit: Royal Field Artillery, then 2nd Battalion, Royal Fusiliers (City of London Regiment).

It is not known when he enlisted but he was awarded the 1915 Star for service in the Balkans.

Joseph was killed in action at the Battle of the Somme.

He died July 3, 1916 and is commemorated on the Thiepval Memorial, Pier and Face 8C 9A & 16A.

Joseph is also commemorated on the Coxhoe War Memorial, Co. Durham.

Joseph Edwin Johnson is the great uncle of John Malcolm of Newton Aycliffe.

Photographs courtesy of John Malcolm

KENDALL, Robert. b. 1892 in Bishopton, Co. Durham.

Parents: William Kendall from Norfolk and Mary J. Milligan from Belfast.

Family: Robert married Cicely Mary Goundry December 12, 1914. Cicely was the sister of Henry Goundry, whose name is on the War Memorial at Aycliffe. 2 daughters, Gertrude Mary, born 1915 and Constance Ruby, born 1920.

Army number: 1541. Rank: Corporal.

Unit: 19th Battalion, Durham Light Infantry.

Attested: August 7, 1915 at Bishop Auckland. He was 23 years 8 months old. He was living at Heighington Street, Aycliffe. Robert was a miner. Robert was 5' ½" and weighed 106 lbs.

Robert was posted October 30, 1915 and was sent to France April 21, 1916. By January 28, 1916 Robert was promoted to Lance Corporal and then Corporal July 22, 1916. By this time he had been transferred to the 2/7th Manchesters with the new number 77785.

Robert received a gunshot wound in his left thigh October 20, 1916 and then 4 days later a gunshot wound in his left loin and back and was sent back to England. He was discharged from hospital December 13, 1916.

June 2, 1917 Robert embarked at Folkestone. December 12, 1917 he was transferred to the Tank Corps. September 7, 1918 Robert was wounded in action, and a week later he received gunshot wounds to his left hand and thigh. By October 21, 1918 he is at the Tanks Corps Depot at Wareham and was posted to the 19th Battalion Tank Corps November 2, 1918.

Robert received his Protection Certificate December 19, 1918.

Robert Kendall is the grandfather of Mrs Hodge of Darlington, who has kindly provided the photographs.

Robert Kendall, front row, 2nd left

Robert Kendall, stood back left

KENT, Harold Leslie. b. 1894 in Aycliffe.

Parents: Charles Kent and Hannah Wilkinson.

Wife: Jane Ann Wake.

Children: Lily, born 1914 and Harold Leslie, born 1918.

1911 census: family lived in the High Street, Aycliffe. Charles was a butcher and his sons (Harold) Leslie and Joseph were his assistants.

Army number: 204390. Rank: Private.

Unit: 4th Battalion, Northumberland Fusiliers.

Harold Leslie Kent with wife Jane Ann and daughter Lily.
Photograph courtesy Lesley Walton.

KENT, George Edmund. b. 1897, brother of Harold Leslie above.

Army number: 46322. Rank: Sergeant. Unit: 79 Royal Engineers.

AYCLIFFE SAPPER HONOURED

Aycliffe residents will be glad to learn that Sapper George E. Kent, R.E., third son of Mr. and Mrs. Charles Kent of that village, has been awarded parchment for gallant conduct and devotion to duty in the field. The transcript reads as follows, and is signed by the Major-General commanding the division —"I have read with great pleasure a report of your regimental commander and brigade commander regarding gallant conduct and devotion to duty in the field on 1 July, 1916."

Bombardier J. Spencer, R.F.A., Bridge-st., Haverton Hill, near Middlesbrough, has been awarded the Military Medal.

Sapper George Edmund Kent was honoured for his gallant conduct and devotion to duty on July 1, 1916.

Article dated Tuesday, 5 December, 1916.

With kind permission of The Northern Echo.

Lochnagar Crater, La Boiselle
result of explosion
July 1, 1916

KENT, Alfred Joseph. b. 1895 in Aycliffe.

Parents: Thomas Kent and Mary Carrick.

Alfred is the brother of John Walter and Norman Kent below.

Alfred enlisted in the Royal Naval Air Service.

Service number: 252695. Rank. Airman.

Alfred sent postcards back home.

Alfred married Norah Wake in 1918 and died in 1953.

Alfred is the father of Mrs Joan Davies of Aycliffe.

Photograph and card courtesy of Mrs Joan Davies

KENT, John Walter. b. February 28, 1898 in Aycliffe.

Army number: 178498. Rank: Private. Unit: Machine Gun Corps.

John was a clerk working for N.E.R. He was 18 years and 5 months old.

His dispersal certificate is dated January 11, 1920, North Camp, Ripon.

John Walter Kent died in 1969.

KENT, (James) Norman. b. 1900 in Aycliffe.

Unit: unknown.

KENT, James Cecil. b. November 30, 1895 in Aycliffe.

Parents: Christopher and Elizabeth Ann Kent.

Family: four brothers and sisters in the 1911 census.

James married Emma Doran in 1920 and had 3 children.

Army number: 36563. Rank: Private.

Unit: 3rd Battalion, Durham Light Infantry.

Medals: Victory and British Medal.

Photograph courtesy of Beryl Wilson of Darlington

War

Where will I be tomorrow?

Still stuck in the trenches?

Wish I was home once more

Where I belong

Screams from the wounded

Lying on the ground.

Blood, Blood and death everywhere

I can take no more

"God just kill me now!"

BANG! BANG!

My pain has ended

I am a spirit now.

Leah Hughes and Elisha Simpson, aged 10

Aycliffe Village Primary School

LAMB, Robert Robson. b. 1895 in Gateshead, Co. Durham.

Parents: Thomas Scott Lamb and Mary Robson.

1911 census: the family was living at 110, Raby Street, Gateshead. Robert had 4 sisters and an elder brother, also called Thomas Scott Lamb. Robert was working as a pony driver in the coal mine.

Attested: November 15, 1915 at Gateshead. Robert was 19 years 355 days old and was now a carriage oiler. His address was now 20, Northbourne Street, Gateshead. Robert was 5' 7 ½" tall and weighed 125 lbs.

Army number: 21/270. Rank: Private.

Unit: 21st Battalion then 18th Battalion, Durham Light Infantry.

Robert went to France May 29, 1916 and was posted to the 18th Battalion.

Robert received a gunshot wound to his left thigh and had a compound fracture of his femur September 23, 1917. He became dangerously ill and died September 25, 1917 at 19 C.C. S. France.

Robert is buried at Duisans British Cemetery, Etrun, Grave V. B. 23.

Robert's possessions were sent to his father September 8, 1919. These were letters, photos, cards, note book, purse, 2 pencils, 3 badges, 2 numerals, brooch, small crucifix, 2 pieces of shrapnel, wallet and a gold ring. Robert's father received his medals in 1920 and 1921.

Robert Robson Lamb is the uncle of Mr Watson of Aycliffe.

LAX, John Willie. b. 1892 in Aycliffe.

Parents: William and Ellen Lax of 53, Lowson Street, Darlington.

Family: wife Florence Annie Hill, daughter Doris.

Army number: 18530. Rank: Corporal. Unit: 13th Service Battalion, Forest of Dean Pioneers, Gloucestershire Regiment.

1911 census: John Willie Lax, married 2 years, living with his wife and year old daughter at 14, Gregson Street, Sacriston, Durham. John Willie Lax was 29, a Miner Bricklayer working at the colliery. His wife, Florence Annie Hill, was 26, born Toft Hill, Durham, and his daughter, Doris was 1 year old, born Sacriston.

Killed in Action: died of wounds April 27, 1918, age 36.

Buried: Boulogne Eastern Cemetery, Pas de Calais, France, Grave Ref. IX. A. 37.

With kind permission of the Evening Despatch,

LAX.—Died of wounds in France, April 27th, 1918, Corporal Jack Lax, Gloucestershire Regt., aged 36, late Scoutmaster, 1st Sacriston Troop, dearly-beloved husband of Florence Lax, and youngest son of the late William Lax and of Ellen Lax, 53, Lowson-street, Darlington. Deeply mourned by his loving wife and daughter, mother, brothers, sisters, father and mother-in-law, and family. Loved by all.

LEADBITTER, Joseph. b. 1877 in Blackhill, Co. Durham.

Army number: 677.

Rank: Private.

Unit: 6th Battalion, Durham Light Infantry.

Joseph is on the right of the middle row.

Photograph courtesy of Edmund Leadbitter.

Parents: Joseph and Amelia Leadbitter.

1891 census: Joseph was 14 and working as a general labourer in the ironworks.

1901 census: Joseph was living with his wife with his in-laws, William and Dianah Skelton, in Consett.

1911 census: Joseph had been married 11 years and had 2 children, William, age 8 and Joseph, age 2. Joseph was working as a steel smelter.

July 4, 1908 Joseph rejoined the Territorial Army, Private 677, 6th Battalion, Durham Light Infantry. He was 31 years, 3 months old. He lived at 54, Edith Street, Consett. He had previously served in the 2nd Battalion, Durham Light Infantry from February 2, 1904 to March 31, 1908.

Joseph had trained annually from 1908. He was embodied August 5, 1914. Joseph arrived at Boulogne April 19, 1915.

October 21, 1916 Joseph was released for munition work at Consett Iron Company.

March 10, 1917 Joseph was discharged on health grounds. He was 40 years and 3 months old. Joseph was 5' 5" tall, sallow complexion, and he had brown eyes and black hair.

Joseph Leadbitter is the grandfather of Edmund Leadbitter of Aycliffe.

Durham Light Infantry badge courtesy Bill Lowery

Annie Leafe, centre back row, 6th from left

LEAFE, Annie. b. July 17, 1895 in Kirk Deighton, Yorkshire.

Parents: George Leafe and Annie Shelton.

Unit: Land Army.

As early as October 1914 Annie was working at Ambleside, lodging with a Mrs Ellis at Red Bank, Ambleside.

Annie sent many postcards to her siblings and her future brother in law, Herbert Grainger and his sister Ada. A postcard Ada Grainger sent to Annie in October, 1914, says that there were many Belgians in Harrogate. Another postcard received from her friend Barbara in December 1914 says that there were 3,000 soldiers in Harrogate.

Annie Leafe is the great aunt of David Ellis of Newton Aycliffe. David supplied the photograph of Annie, and the postcard below sent by Herbert Grainger from France June 1, 1915 to Annie.

LEE, Henry Stephen. b. December 26, 1890 in Torquay, Devon.

Parents: James Lee and Edith Pascoe.

Henry travelled alone to the United States when he was 17 years old. He worked his way across America.

1912 Henry was injured while working for the Wright brothers. He lost the sight in his right eye.

Attested: July 25, 1917 in Vancouver.

Rank: Sapper. Unit: Canadian Expeditionary Force.

He travelled back to Liverpool on the SS Metagama, then on to France.

Henry was honourably discharged August 11, 1919 in London.

Henry's eldest son James married Maria Bowerbank from Cornforth and they lived in Newton Aycliffe for over 40 years.

Henry Stephen Lee's grandson and great-grandchildren still live in Newton Aycliffe.

Henry Stephen Lee and Ada Moore on their wedding day, April 26, 1919.

Photograph courtesy of Joyce Malcolm

LEE, Patrick J. b. 1898 in Coundon.

Parents: Patrick and Esther Lee.

Army number: 988846. Rank: Private. Unit: MGA.

Patrick is the father of George Lee of School Aycliffe.

LENG, John Robert. b. 1888 in Pity Me, Co. Durham.

Parents: James Jordan Leng and Ann Johnson.

1911 census: the family were at Broom Park, Durham. There had been 10 children but 4 had died. One of John's sisters was Ethel Leng, who married John Parker in 1919.

John Robert was known as Jack.

John's medal card survives.

He was Private 62365 Royal Welch Fusiliers, then 14210 Border Regiment, then 40174 Loyal North Lancashire Regiment and finally Royal Engineers 353951.

LENG, James. b. 1890 in Pity Me.

Brother of John above.

James Leng's war service records have not survived.

John Robert and James Leng are great uncles of Mrs Willis of Newton Aycliffe.

Photographs courtesy of Mrs Willis

Bomb at roadside, Beaumont-Hamel

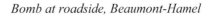

10

WAR! WAR! Why does it exist?

Hatred, sorrow and death is not a wish!

WAR! WAR! Why is it to be?

Scared depression and anger;

These are the feeling that a soldier has.

WAR! WAR! why does it exist?

Hatred, sorrow and death is not a wish

WAR! WAR! Why is it to be?

Cards, fags and carving too:

These are the things the soldiers do.

Wire tags and letters too:

These are the things that are important to you.

BANG! BANG! that is all you hear;

Quick! Quick! the enemies are here!

GAS! GAS! The bells are ringing!

QUICK! QUICK! or we will be digging!

WAR! WAR! why does it exist?

Hatred, sorrow and death is not a wish.

WAR! WAR! why is it to be?

RATS! RATS! the vermin they are,

easy to trick, but *we* aren't!

WAR! WAR! why does it exist?

Hatred, sorrow and death is not a wish

WAR! WAR! why is it to be?

BRITZ and the Fritz fighting

From Spring until Winter

1915 is nearly here.

WAR! WAR! each day like a year;

Over the top and you'll be clear!

Jordan Bambridge, Kyle O'Donnell
and Alex Harrison

Greenfield Community College

Now you know what happened.

This is the truth.

LEWIS, Nicholas. b. June 4, 1883 in Coundon Grange, Co. Durham.

Parents: John Lewis, born Ireland, and Elizabeth Clarke, whose father Nicholas was born in Ireland.

Nicholas and his brother Robert are with their maternal grandparents in 1891 and 1901.

In the 1911 census Nicholas is living with his brother Robert, who now is married to Mary Jane Briddick from South Church. He was a labourer in the saw mills.

There is a medal card for a Nicholas Lewis, Private 23756, Northumberland Fusiliers. It states he had been discharged.

Nicholas had been gassed in the trenches and was fully pensioned from the army during the war.

Nicholas married Emma Milner in 1918.

Nicholas was found dead in the Hollywood bog area of Byers Green, reported in the Evening Despatch for Tuesday, April 21, 1925. A coroner's report found that his death was due to exposure accelerated by loss of blood from a wound on his face.

Nicholas Lewis is the great, great grandfather of Euan Fitzgerald of Aycliffe.

WAR!

Soldiers sharing everything

Fags and food from home sweet home,

Sharing life in a trench

Not so bad when you have friends -

Comrades sharing the relentless lice

Sharing beds with ear nibbling rats

Sharing pain

Sharing death.

Euan Fitzgerald, aged 11

Aycliffe Village Primary School

LIDDLE, John. b. 1895 at Coxhoe, Co. Durham.

Parents: Thomas and Margaret Liddle.

Army number: 2491. Rank: Private.

Unit: 1/5th Battalion, Durham Light Infantry.

John died May 24, 1915, age 20, at the Battle of Bellewaarde Ridge.

John is commemorated on the Menin Gate, Ypres, Panel 36 & 38.

John is also commemorated on the Coxhoe War Memorial, Co. Durham.

John Liddle is a paternal relative of Joyce Malcolm of Newton Aycliffe.

Menin Gate, Ypres

Coxhoe War Memorial

Photographs courtesy of Joyce Malcolm

LOCKIE, William Raymond. b. July 15, 1901 in Aycliffe.

Parents: William Lockie and Barbara Tarbit.

1911 census: the family was living at 20, Armstrong Court, Saltwell Road, Benshaw, Gateshead. William Lockie senior was a Railway Signalman. William junior was the youngest of 3 brothers.

In the 1918 Absent Voters' List for Great Aycliffe, William was living at Monks' End, Aycliffe, while his brothers are living at North Aycliffe.

Army number: 39137. Rank: Private. Unit: Army Service Corps.

LOCKIE, Thomas James. b. 1897 in Haughton Lane, Durham. Older brother of William above.

Army number: 309287. Rank: Private. Unit: Royal Engineers.

LOCKIE, George. Brother of William and Thomas above.

Army number: 911507. Rank: Private. Unit: 46 Canadians.

LOCKIE, Edwin Charles. Brother of William Thomas and George above.

Army number: 312562. Rank: Pioneer. Unit: I.W. Docks, Royal Engineers.

Lewis Kilding, 8ROY

Greenfield Community College, WW Boxes

LOWERY, Thomas. b. 1894 in Byers Green, Co. Durham.

Parents: Thomas Lowery and Elizabeth Dawson.

Wife: married Alice Ann Waterworth 1915.

1911 census: the family were at 3, Busty Terrace, Byers Green Colliery. Thomas was working as a coal miner putter.

Attested: September 3, 1914 at Bishop Auckland Town Hall.

Army number: 235054. Rank: Private.

Unit: Durham Light Infantry, then the 7th Battalion, Border Regiment, The Royal Garrison Artillery and The King's (Liverpool) Regiment.

August 3, 1915 Thomas joined The King's Own Royal Lancaster Regiment, which fought at the Battle of the Somme. Thomas was wounded in the battle.

Thomas fought at the Battle of Pilkem Ridge, July 31, 1917 and at the Battle of the Menin Road Ridge, September 20, 1917.

Thomas then fought in the Battle of Cambrai November 20, 1917, where he was captured and spent the rest of the war as a prisoner. He escaped November 5, 1918, 6 days before the end of the war.

Thomas Lowery, stood middle row on right in the photograph above, is the grandfather of Bill Lowery of Newton Aycliffe, who has given the photographs and information.

LOWERY, Thomas, D.C.M. b. 1892.

Parents: John A. Lowery and Catherine Redhead. Cousin of Thomas Lowery above.

Wife: May Barrett, living at 7, Wylam Terrace, Shield Row, West Stanley, Co. Durham.

Attested: February 1915.

Rank: 2nd Lieutenant.

Unit: 15th Battalion, Durham Light Infantry.

Thomas was wounded at the Battle of the Somme, July 1, 1916.

Thomas was killed August 3, 1917, age 25. He is buried in Croiselles British Cemetery, Pas de Calais, Grave I. B.23.

THE LATE MR. JOHN LOWERY.

A report of the funeral of Mr. Lowery will be fixed on Page 2.

Thomas Lowery, above and his father John. John's obituary appeared in the Country Chronicle, July 26, 1917 and Thomas's obituary appeared August 9, 1917.

MARR, William Lisle. b. 1891 at South View, Kelloe, Co. Durham.

Parents: Thomas Marr and Ellen Carr.

1911 census: the family was at 52, South View, Kelloe. William's mother had died. William was 20 and worked as a coal filler.

Unit: unknown.

William served in WW1 and survived. He was the brother of June Palmer's grandmother, Ethel Marr.

11300 Sergeant James Marshall DCM.

6TH and 1/5th Battalions, East Lancashire Regiment.

*Photograph courtesy of
Margaret Harrison*

MARSHALL, James, D.C.M. b. Lancashire.

Army number: 11300. Rank: Sergeant.

Unit: 6th and 1/5th Battalions, East Lancashire Regiment.

The citation for the Distinguished Conduct Medal, published in the London Gazette September, 1918.

"11300 Sergt. J. Marshall, E. Lanc. R. (Burnley) This N.C.O. took charge of his platoon when the commander had been killed, and moved forward to a position that was being attacked by the enemy. Though troops in the line were falling back, he kept his men together and held the position until he was ordered to withdraw eight hours later, though during most of the time his right flank was quite unsupported. His intelligent grip of the tactical situation and his gallant conduct were of the greatest value."

James Marshall is the grandfather of Margaret Harrison of Newton Aycliffe.

George Scaife, 8ROY

*Greenfield Community College,
WW1 Boxes*

MARSHALL, Moor. b. 1889 in Darlington, Co. Durham.

Parents: Moor Marshall and Caroline Willis, who married 1878.

1881 census: his father was working as a railway guard in Darlington, and in the 1901 census he had moved to Heighington Street, Aycliffe, and was a railway agent.

1911 census: Moor senior had become Railway Station Master, still living in Heighington Street. Moor Marshall junior was working as a County Council Clerk. June 1916 he married Frances Iceton.

Army number: 2157. Rank: A/Sergeant. Unit: Royal Army Medical Corps.

MARSHALL, Sydney. b. 1897 in Darlington. Brother of Moor above.

Army number: 34313. Rank: Private. Unit: Royal Army Medical Corps.

MARSHALL, Gordon Osborne. Brother of Moor and Sydney above.

Army number: 158314. Rank: Private. Unit: R.F.C.

RAMC badges courtesy David Ellis

MATSON, Thomas. b. 1889 in Aycliffe.

Parents: William Matson, born in Morden, and Mary Ann Robinson, born in Aycliffe. Mary Ann was the daughter of Jarvis Robinson. They lived at Heworth Cottage, Aycliffe.

Army number: 6564. Rank: Gunner. Unit: 151st (Darlington) Heavy Battery Corps.

Attested: November 6, 1915. Thomas lived at Heworth Cottage, Aycliffe, and was 22 years 4 months old. He was 5' 7" tall, and had a chest measurement of 38.4 inches with a range of 2 ½ inches.

Thomas served in England November 6, 1915 to June 18, 1916. He was in France June 19 to October 1, 1917 and then in England October 2, 1917 to November 21, 1918.

His character was very good. Thomas received a weekly pension of 8/3 (42p), to be reviewed November 25, 1919, for 30% disability.

MATSON, William Jervis. b. 1894 in Aycliffe. Brother of Thomas above.

Unit: unknown.

MAUDE, Robert Henry. b. 1897 in Annfield Plain, Co. Durham.

Parents: William Henry Maude and Elizabeth Foster.

1911 census: the family were at 3, Johnson Terrace, Annfield Plain. Robert had 3 siblings, Caroline, Lydia and Catherine.

Army number: 7762, then 203172. Rank: Private. Unit: 1st/4th Battalion, Yorkshire Regiment.

Robert enlisted at Sunderland.

Robert was killed in action April 23, 1917. Robert was 21 years old. He is buried in the L'Homme Mort British Cemetery, Ecoust-St. Mein, Grave II. A.16.

Robert Henry Maude is the uncle of Betty Elliot of Newton Aycliffe.

Kyra Marshall, 8ROY

Greenfield Community College, WW1 Boxes

Timeline 1918

March 21: Germans launch 1st of a series of offensives on Western Front.

April 9: Battle of Vimy Ridge involving Canadian Forces.

April 21: Von Richthofen, the "Red Baron", killed in action.

July 18: Allied counter attack begins.

September 11: Allies break Hindenburg defence line.

October 1: Ludendorff asks parliament to make peace.

October 30: Turkey signs armistice.

November 3: Austria signs armistice.

11th hour of 11th day of 11th month Armistice on the Western Front.

MAUGHAN, Peter. b. 1888 in Leasingthorne, Co. Durham.

Parents: Peter and Mary Jane Maughan.

1911 census: the family were living at 5, Oak Terrace, Leasingthorne. Peter was 23 and doing shift work. The following year, 1912, Peter married Margaret Hannah Henderson, and lived at 24, Front Street, Kirk Merrington, Co. Durham.

Army number: 19266. Rank: Private. Unit: 7th Battalion, East Yorkshire Regiment.

Peter served from October 7, 1915.

Peter was killed in action August 12, 1918. He is commemorated at the Heath Cemetery, Harbonnières, south of Albert, Grave II. B.3.

Peter Maughan is the great uncle of Judith Wilson of Newton Aycliffe.

MAYNE, Joseph M. b. June 9, 1897, Framwellgate Moor.

Parents: Henry and Catherine Mayne. 1911 census the family were living in 142, Newcastle Row, Framwellgate Moor.

Army number: 82282. Rank: Signaller.

Units: Royal Horse & Royal Field Artillery.

Attested: August 10, 1914. Joseph was 18 years 2 months old. September 11, 1914 he was posted to the 161 Battery.

Originally listed as a Driver, he was later promoted to Gunner, 412 Battery August 20, 1917, and finally Signaller.

From correspondence to his parents Belgium, France and Mesopotamia (now part of Iraq) were some of the countries where Joe saw service. While in France his sister had written to say that Joseph had not had any leave since being in France. This letter was received July 26, 1916.

Joseph served in France May 10, 1915 to May 2, 1917. He was home May 2, 1917 to September 27, 1917. Joseph was then in Egypt September 28 to January 1, 1919. He was then on board a ship January 29, 1919 to February 24, 1919, then home February 25, 1919 to March 31, 1920.

Following his transfer to the Army Reserve on April 10, 1919, Joe returned to civilian life, working as a coal hewer at Kimblesworth Colliery and Cocken Drift among other pits.

Joseph Mayne is the grandfather of Terry Barron of Newton Aycliffe.

Photographs and postcards courtesy of Terry Barron

McNALLY, William. b. 1895 in Ryhope, Durham.

Parents: William and Ellen McNally, both born in Sunderland. William had 7 siblings.

Army number: 95281. Rank: Private.

Unit: 1/9th Battalion, Durham Light Infantry.

On William's Protection Certificate of October 23, 1919, his home address is 12, Railway Street, Murton Colliery.

William McNally is the father of Ruby Adamson of Newton Aycliffe

*The photograph right is dated 9th DLI, Rhineland, 1918.
The newspaper held is The Times on the day the war ended.*

Photograph courtesy of Ruby Adamson.

The Night And Day

As I walk through the trenches,

I think about my family,

Back at home.

Darkness falls,

Supper goes round,

Darkness lasts.

Early in the morning war starts again.

I could see the men drop down,

Others running around.

Hand in hand with death.

I wish the days and nights would pass by...

Lucas Pilling, aged 11 and Annie Self, aged 10

MUIR, Arthur Frederick. b. November 26, 1888 in Newcastle.

Parents: John Muir of Glasgow and Jane Peddie of Holy Island, Northumberland.

Arthur's father was an engine fitter in 1901. By 1911 he was an agent, living in Linthorpe Road, Middlesbrough. He had had 8 children, 1 of whom had died by 1911, as had his wife Jane.

Arthur married Quadrownia Fanny Fewster at Stockton in 1914 and they lived in Norton. Arthur was a motor engineer.

Service number: 16776. Rank: Pilot Officer. Unit: Royal Flying Corps.

Arthur flew the Avro DH6, BE 2c, 2e &12, and Sopwith Bomber. He was mentioned for valuable services.

After the war Arthur worked in India for a maharajah. He died in 1965.

MUIR, Percy. b. 1895 Ellesmere Port, Cheshire. Brother of Arthur above.

Army number: 3080. Rank: Private. Unit: 1st/5th Battalion, Durham Light Infantry.

Attested: April 17, 1915.

Percy was killed September 18, 1916, age 21. His name is on the Thiepval Memorial, Pier and Face 14 A and 15 C.

Death Plaque of Percy Muir

Courtesy of Heather Lawson

Arthur and Percy Muir are the great uncles of Heather Lawson of Brafferton.

11

45 Queen Street,

Durham,

1st September 1914.

Dear Ryan,

     This is the first letter of many I shall send to you. We are all very proud of you here in Durham and hope you are well. Little Oliver is missing his Daddy so much and is waiting for you to arrive home. Mary is extremely worried about Big Tony as he has not replied to any of her letters; could you please inform me in your next letter how he is doing - for Mary.

Your father is fine and his business is doing well at the minute with the war and all. I love you so much and hope that you are in good health. I am looking forward to your reply and we are all wishing you well. Write soon.

Lucia x

45 Queen Street,

Durham

12th September 1914

Dear Ryan,

I hope you have received my previous letter, since I have not had a reply. I hope you are coping with the loss of your brother. I received a telegram yesterday stating his loss and was unsure why you have not told me yourself. I have informed Mary about Tony's death and she is in a   sequence of mourning process-es. Oliver is asking how his daddy is and is missing you dearly.

I have been looking after the house well, but I am falling behind on the bills. After you left work to join the army we haven't had enough money to cope. Oliver is going to your mother's for a while, until I can catch up on payments. If not we may have to move out.

I am going to work for a while, instead of being a house wife, and your parents are cooking meals for us. I am going to work at the Grand Hall as a maid; the pay isn't the best, but hopefully we will make it through.

I have also written this letter to tell you about the death of your father, Ben. I didn't want to tell you as soon, as I knew you would be busy fighting. Doctors haven't diagnosed him with   anything and they suspect he died of old age.

He died peacefully in his bed and is now at rest. At least we now know he will be free of any pain he kept from us. His funeral is on the 2nd of October and I hope that you will be back in time to put your father to rest. Mary is worried about you as she doesn't want to lose another family member. I'm sorry for giving you most of the bad news in one letter, but hopefully the rest of my letters will bring you good news. We are trying to postpone Oliver's christening until you get back, so we are hoping to have it in late November.

We miss you so much here in Durham and we are all so proud of you. We all wish you all the best. Please reply soon and relieve me of my worries.

Take care,

Lucia x

Dear Ryan,

We are all so worried about you- why haven't you written back? I haven't received a telegram, so you must have a good reason. I was hoping you would return in time for your father's funeral, however you did not. It was so morbid - only Mary and some colleagues came. We had only just recovered from Tony's funeral at the time, so it was too hard for Mary…

Then of course there is the funeral for Oliver.

I am so, so sorry Ryan. He was diagnosed with scarlet fever, and there was nothing we could do. It was all so quick, Ryan. I am coping with the grief… I am trying. I suppose it will all catch up with me at once sometime in the future.

Please come home, Ryan. That's what he would want. The family send their love, take care.

Lucia x

Nicole Todd, Scarlet Findlay and Katie Oliver

Greenfield Community College

NELSON, William. b. 1877 in Aycliffe.

Family: wife Mary E. Nelson, son Harry Nelson, born 1900. They lived in Orlands in the 1901 census.

Unit: unknown.

NELSON, Harry. b. 1900 in Aycliffe.

Unit: unknown.

NELSON, Harry.

Wife: Annie Mary Burnside. They had a son, Thomas Robert Farmery Nelson in 1915.

Unit: unknown.

NELSON, William. b. 1892 at Heighington Station.

Parents: Henry and Annie Nelson were living at Heighington Street, Aycliffe in the 1911 census.

Army number: 46325. Rank: Private. Unit: 9 Signal Corps..

NELSON, Alick. b. 1894 at Heighington Station. Brother of William above.

Unit: unknown.

OAKLEY, George. b. 1885 in Hyson, Nottingham.

Parents: William and Mary Oakley.

George is the elder brother of Arthur and Harold.

Attested: November 27, 1915 in Matlock, Derbyshire.

Army number: 312441. Rank: Private. Unit: Tank Corps.

George was called up September 3, 1918 and demobilized September 25, 1919.

George is the grandfather of George Oakley of Newton Aycliffe and great uncle of Brian Oakley of Canada.

OAKLEY, Arthur. b. 1892 in Holloway, Derbyshire.

Arthur and his younger brother Harold emigrated to Canada in 1910.

Arthur attested April 5, 1916 at Empress, Alberta. He had originally attested to the 212th Canadian Americans but this was broken up to strengthen the Princess Patricia's Canadian Light Infantry.

Army number: 261154. Rank: Private.

Unit: 2nd Division, Canadian Expeditionary Force, Princess Patricia's Canadian Light Infantry.

Photographs of George and Arthur courtesy of Brian Oakley

Arthur arrived at Liverpool November 21, 1916. In France he fought in the first wave of assault at Vimy Ridge. The PPCLI were central and hidden in Grange Tunnel.

Arthur was wounded 4 times: first a gunshot wound to the forehead, 2 shrapnel wounds to his back and legs, and finally by a mustard gas shell. He was blinded and unable to speak for 2 months. Arthur spent more than a year recovering, primarily at Lord Derby Military Hospital (for respiratory conditions) just north of Warrington. Here he met Lucy Algie, who became his wife.

The only decoration Arthur would wear was a small after-service lapel pin "For service at the front". He received 2 service medals.

Arthur is remembered in Christ Church, Holloway.

Arthur Oakley is the grandfather of Brian Oakley of Canada, who has kindly sent the information and photographs about his grandfather and great uncles.

OAKLEY, Harold. b. May 28, 1896 in Holloway, Derbyshire. Brother of George and Arthur.

Army number: 105122. Rank: Private.

Unit: 16th Battalion, Canadian Scottish (Princess Mary's Own) Regiment.

Attested: November 4, 1915 in Regina, Saskatchewan (near Fosters of Abernethy). He joined the Canadian Over-seas Expeditionary Force

Harold was living at Arbernethy, Saskatchewan. He was a farmer.

He was 5' 9 ¾" tall, had a dark complexion, and brown eyes and hair. His brother George was named as his next of kin.

Harold arrived in England August 14, 1916.

From a letter it says he went to Smedley's Mill in Holloway in his Scots uniform, kilt and tam. Neither his brother George, nor his father William recognized him.

Photographs courtesy of Brian Oakley

The 16th Battalion were in a line west of Courcelette to attack the Regina Trench.

Harold died of his wounds at the No. 9 Casualty Clearing Station, September 27, 1916.

Harold is buried at Contay British Cemetery, Grave II. D.3.

This cemetery is 2 miles west of Warloy-Baillon and 7 ¼ miles west of Albert, France.

Harold is commemorated in Christ Church, Holloway and on the WW1 Memorial, Long Lane, Holloway.

OATES, Percy Edmundson. b. 1894 in St. Helens Auckland, Co. Durham.

Parents: John Oates, born 1838 in St. Helens Auckland, and Agnes Thirwall, born 1858 in Whitehaven. They ran the sub-post office in St. Helens.

Army number: 118837. Rank: Private. Unit: Army Auxiliary Corps.

Percy Oates attested August 16, 1915. He was 21 years old, 5' 11" tall, weighed 166 lbs, chest 39". His next of kin is entered as his mother, Agnes Oates, of 11, Highfield Terrace, Bishop Auckland.

He embarked at Southampton September 30, 1915, arriving at Rouen the next day aboard the SS King Edward. He was attached to 589 Horse Transport Company, 1st. Army Auxiliary H. T. Coy. January 18, 1916, he was admitted to hospital but re-joined his company 3 days later, January 21, 1916.

March 1, 1918, Percy had a temporary transfer to 1st Army Buses and returned to his company in April, 1918. He was appointed L/Corporal (unpaid) May 15, 1918 and then as Established L/Corporal September 13, 1918.

November 5, 1918, he was sent to 928 Asia Art. Ei. Company.

OATES, Robert Storey. b. May 22, 1896, St. Helens Auckland, Co. Durham, died in September, 1978. Brother of Percy above.

Unit: Royal Engineers.

Robert Storey Oates is indicated on the right and is on the right in the second photograph.

Photographs courtesy of Alan Oates.

Robert Storey Oates is the father of Alan Oates, Churchwarden of St. Andrew's Church, Aycliffe.

O'NEILL, Patrick. b. 1887 in Belfast.

Army number: 13673. Rank: Private.

Unit: 7th Battalion, Royal Scot Fusiliers.

Patrick married Lizzie Flannigan about September, 1907 in Belfast.

Family: 3 children, Elizabeth, James Patrick, born October 3, 1911, and Margaret.

Patrick probably was based at Port Glasgow. He went to France July 10, 1915.

Killed in Action: September 26, 1915. Patrick was killed at the Battle of Hill 70 according to the Remembrance Card below.

Commemorated at the Loos Memorial, north west of Lens, Panel 46-49. Patrick is also named in Ireland's Memorial Records.

Patricia Montgomery, granddaughter of Patrick O'Neill, kindly supplied photographs and information. Patricia lives in Newton Aycliffe.

In loving Remembrance

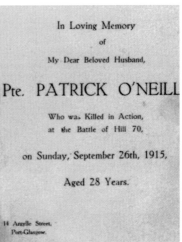

In Loving Memory
of
My Dear Beloved Husband,

Pte. PATRICK O'NEILL

Who was Killed in Action,
at the Battle of Hill 70,

on Sunday, September 26th, 1915,

Aged 28 Years.

14 Argylle Street,
Port-Glasgow.

12

To my dearest wife Lily and children Ronan, Caitlin and Charlotte,

I write to you bearing bad news.

Time is burning out like the remaining flame of a candle and I cannot bear not saying Goodbye to you before my last breath. I have no regrets about fighting for my King and Country, for   protecting my family. Maybe that is my pride speaking, but I don't care about that now; there are more important things to write about than an old dying fool's pride! That is the awful truth my dearest, this terrible war will be the end of me.

I wish you could be here with me, however I know this is selfish. No wife or child should have to go through that traumatic experience – and I would never wish it of mine. I want the children to remember me as I was, if they remember at all.

At that moment my soul will travel from this world to the next, maybe to heaven if I am lucky. The sound of gun shots echoes and nearly shatters my ear drums. Bomb shells rain, whistling as they go and as their weight hits the ground, they explode, killing men in their deadly debris.

I wish I could see our beautiful daughters grow up to look just like you. I hope our son becomes a brave warrior and protects you and the girls better than I protected you. Don't worry my love, death has me in his grip; I won't have to bear this horror much longer.

Please remember me for my courage and for how much I love you. Tell the children that their Daddy will be watching over them through thick and thin.

With all my love,

Charles, Daddy

***

Bombs whistle overhead while men flee for their lives, screaming as they run. One man drags himself through the debris clutching his side all the while. The wasted blood flows from the pulsing wound, drying and caking itself to his deadly white skin. The aching soon changes to a sharp pain, momentarily stopping his progress towards the safety of the trench. Lying in his own pool of blood, he is dying from his wounds. A distressed officer hurries past; glancing out of the corner of his eye he spots a man. The man breathes one word before giving up to the darkness that wants to consume him: 'Help…'

Waking to the bright light of the rising sun, his awful experience seems to be nothing but a dream. Except for the ache which still clings to his side. Maybe he will believe it was just a nightmare, however that pain, which never goes away, will remind him.

The smells of death and blood overwhelm him. Screams and cries echo through the wards of the hospital. But it is when the relatives come that the pain in his heart hits its peak. People come and go from day to day, never leaving any trace. For months he stares into nothingness, silently crying for help.

It was on that day that they told him; his life in this war had been played out. Placing a pen and paper in his hand, he hung onto it with a death grip and began to write …

'To my dearest wife …..'

Eleanor Atkinson, Lucy Cummings, Mia Bell and Charlotte Klapdor

Greenfield Community College

PALMER, William. b. 1891 at Sidegate, Framwellgate, Durham.

Parents: William Palmer and Ellen Mary Bateson.

1911 census: the family were at 4, Sidegate. William was 19 and working as an assistant in a confectioner's shop.

William served in the Green Howards in WW1, becoming a sergeant.

William is the father-in-law of June Palmer of Aycliffe.

PALMER, William Long. b. 1894 in Sunderland, Co. Durham. He was baptized May 30, 1894 at Monk Wearmouth.

Parents: Isaac Palmer and Mary Ann Long.

1901 census: the family were at 193, Shipley Street, Byker, Newcastle upon Tyne.

1911 census: Isaac was a coal miner hewer, and William was an apprentice brass moulder at the Ordnance Works, Parsons. They now lived at 224, Shipley Street.

Attested: November 28, 1915.

Army number: 263371. Rank: Driver.

Unit: Royal Horse and Royal Field Artillery.

William survived the War, going into the reserves June 6, 1919, and was finally discharged in March 31, 1920. William is in a photograph taken at Parsons of Old Timers.

William Long Palmer is the father of Bill Palmer of Newton Aycliffe.

PARKER, James. b. August 10, 1890 in Kendal.

Parents: Richard and Margaret Ann Parker.

Family: wife Elizabeth Robinson of Aycliffe, married June, 1915. Son James, born 1915, and daughters Margaret, born 1918 and Linda Alice, born 1920.

Army number: 4117, then 90039. Rank: Private.

Unit: 5th Battalion, Durham Light Infantry, then Labour Corps.

James worked as a railway labourer.

James joined up in October 1915 and served until November 1918. He was quite badly wounded near Arras, probably in June 1917 and was sent back to the UK to recover from his wounds. James never went back to France and ended his service with the Labour corps.

Died August 30, 1980. Buried at St Andrew's Church, Aycliffe.

James Parker is the grandfather of Alan Pattison.

PARKER, John. b. 1894 in Wallsend, Northumberland.

Parents: William Parker and Alice Dixon.

1911 census: John is living with his elder brother George at Marley Hill. He is working as a farm labourer.

Army number: P/4/062682. Rank: Private.

Unit: Army Service Corps, 41st Remount Squadron.

Attested March 1, 1915. He was 21 years 2 months old, 5' 1" tall and weighed 128 lbs. John was a farmer. His next of kin was an aunt, Ellen Dixon, with whom he lived at 36, Newcastle Street, Brandon Colliery, Co. Durham.

John embarked at Avonmouth March 27, 1915 and disembarked at Alexandria April 14, 1915. John then embarked at Alexandria November 27, 1915 and disembarked at Salonika December 11, 1915, joining the 41st Remount Squadron.

At some stage John was with the Bedfordshire Regiment as he sent a silk postcard of the regimental badge and a message on the reverse to Ethel Leng saying this was the regiment he was in.

September 18, 1918 John was still at Salonika. He had had 21 days leave and had disembarked at Southampton via Cherbourg and Taranto. John finally left Salonika April 30, 1919, sailing via Taranto for the U.K.

John married Ethel Leng 1919.

John Parker is the grandfather of Mrs Willis of Newton Aycliffe.

Photograph and postcard courtesy of Mrs Willis

13

Tired arms tear away the earth.

Muscles found in an unimportant mine,

muscles that were working for money,

now for their lives,

on a field that will change the world.

Such a simple thing is money -,

Although it was the world,

Now we realise that we have lives;

we consider our families.

We see things better when they are not there.

The orange slip came back.

A simple piece of paper,

no more than paper with ink on,

but the shapes that the ink made,

signalled the end of everything.

Every night we rolled the dice,

and got our lucky number.

We woke in morning seeing the devastation

of those who were not so lucky.

Then waited to roll the dice again.

Out of fear I replaced my father,

to save my family

but more myself, from the white feathers.

It was going to be an adventure, a holiday,

But holidays in hell are not fun.

Every day saw the death of thousands.

It was hard seeing so many leave,

but worse were the cries of mourning,

crying for loss, for hatred,

hatred at the unfair world.

Connor Elston

Greenfield Community College

And the world is unfair,

the way the workers starve

and the languid gorge themselves.

But it is the one we live in.

So we all work hard to save it.

But I can't help asking myself,

'Is it really worth it?'

PINKNEY, William, senior. b. 1869 at High Coniscliffe, Durham.

Parents: Thomas Pinkney and Mary Auton. Wife: married Margaret Outhwaite in 1897.

Enlisted: 1888. Rank: Sergeant Major.

Unit: 2nd Battalion, Yorkshire Regiment (Green Howards).

William sailed to India January 1, 1890 and took part in the Tirah Campaign. William was then attached to the Indian Ordnance. After 13 years William was invalided out of the army.

1911 census: he was an army pensioner, working as a gardener in Brafferton. His son **William** had been born in Madras, India in 1901 and his second son, **Cecil George Pinkney**, in Rangoon, Burma, in 1902.

William's wife, Margaret Outhwaite, was the daughter of George and Mary Jane Outhwaite, who lived at the Post Office, Coatham Mundeville in the 1891 census. George Outhwaite worked as a joiner and cartwright as well as being the postmaster.

William Pinkney re-enlisted in August 1914. He was attached to the 7th Battalion, Yorkshire Regiment as Sergeant Major.

1915 William was in France and engaged in trench warfare, mainly in the vicinity of Hill 60. William's health was affected by a gas attack as well as recurring bouts of malaria. He spent some time in Norwich Hospital and was eventually released from active service.

Medals: Long Service, Good Conduct, North-West Frontier Medal with 6 bars, 1914-1915 Star.

William had 2 certificates for exemplary conduct. He died March 21, 1937 at Brafferton.

Military and Masonic honours were accorded William at his funeral March 24, 1937.

Details of William's life are from the thesis of Louisa Wilson *"Annals of Aycliffe, A Parish of the Palatine",* 1927 (with later additions), pages 246 & 247.

All three Pinkney men served in WW1, the sons' units unknown.

PLASKITT, Albert. b. October 3, 1897 in Colburn, Yorkshire.

Parents: Honora Cambage and Luty Plaskitt of North Somercoates, Lincolnshire.

Army number: 235248. Rank: Private. Unit: 1/7 Middlesex Regiment.

Attested: December, 1916. He was 18 years, 8 months old and lived at Station Terrace, Aycliffe. Albert's next of kin was Nora Plaskitt, his mother. Albert worked as a gangman.

Albert was 22 when he was discharged February 25, 1920. He ranked as Class 5 for a Pension, Disability Code 5. He had a gunshot wound (att) to the stomach and an Appindiciting Scar (sic) (Agg), and had 20% Disablement. He was granted this January 1, 1919.

Medals: British War Medal and Victory Medal.

Both Honora and Luty are buried in St. Andrew's Churchyard, Aycliffe. Albert Plaskitt died 1971 at Richmond, Yorkshire.

POTTS, Leonard Vincent. b. September 4, 1873 in Bishop Wearmouth, Sunderland.

Parents: Leonard Vincent Potts and Mary Ann Ryans.

Leonard married Maggie Murray Munro in 1895. In the 1911 census Leonard was living at 3, Shepherd Street, Sunderland. He was 37 and had 5 children. Leonard worked as a postman.

Attested: 1915. Rank: Private 1688 and then 38041.

Unit: 6 Platoon, B Company, 18th Battalion, Durham Light Infantry, and the Rifle Brigade.

Leonard is the grandfather of Mrs Watson of Aycliffe.

Leonard and his wife Maggie and 5 children, Jane, Grace, Maggie Leonard and Elsie

Photographs courtesy of Mrs Watson

Leonard seated 4th left, second row

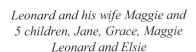

113

QUICKMIRE, James William. b. 1895 in Jarrow.

Parents: James Quickmire and Eliza Ann Freeman, born Darlington.

1901 census: James William Quickmire and his widowed mother Eliza were living at 5, Mechanic Street, Shildon.

Eliza remarried about December, 1901. She married William Sewell and in the 1911 census the family are living at Main Street, Staindrop. James William Quickmire was a coal miner, as was his stepfather.

Army number: 6/2581. Rank: Lance Corporal. Unit: 6th Battalion, Durham Light Infantry.

James was in France June 27, 1915. He was invalided out in May, 1916.

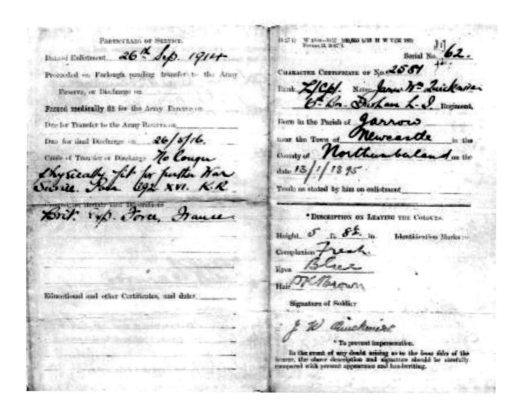

Original document courtesy of Ivor of Aycliffe

RANGECROFT, John Walley.   b. 1896 near Hull, Yorkshire.

Parents: John Robert Rangecroft and Isabel Walley. They had married in York in 1895.

1901 census: John is with his grandparents, George and Ann Rangecroft at 21, Swann Street, York. His grandfather was a railway goods worker, born Bradley Green, Staffordshire.

1911 census: John and two siblings, Constance and Benjamin, are living with their mother and stepfather, George Eshelby at 9, Barron Street, Darlington. George was an engine fitter in the locomotive department of the railway company.

Army number: 21467. Rank: Lance Corporal. Unit: 1st Battalion, Northumberland Fusiliers.

John went to France July 13, 1915. He had formerly been 10091 in the West Yorks Regiment.

Killed in Action May 9, 1916 and buried at Kemmel Chateau Military Cemetery, south west of Ypres, Grave No. 18.

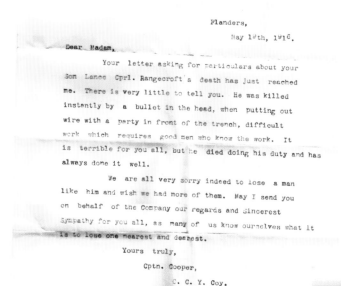

Letter dated May 19, 1916, from Captain Cooper in Flanders describing the death of John Walley Rangecroft:
"Lance Corporal Rangecroft was killed instantly by a bullet in the head, when putting out wire with a party in front of the trench, difficult work which requires good men who know the work."

Medals and Death Plaque of John Walley Rangecroft

Courtesy of Ivor Briggs

John Walley Rangecroft is the brother of the grandmother of Ivor Briggs of Aycliffe.

Brandon Wintour, 8ROY

Greenfield Community College, WW1 Boxes

Olivia Archer, 8GBV

RICHARDSON, George. b. 1888 at Travellers Rest, Aycliffe.

Parents: Joseph Richardson, born at Preston Le Skerne and Annie May, who was born at Cornforth.

1891 census: George was 3 and was living with his parents at Railway Cottages, Sherburn. He had a sister, Mary. His father was a railway labourer.

1901 census: the family were still at Railway Cottages, though there were now two more sons, Joseph, age 9, and William, age 2, and Joseph's mother Alice, age 82. She was born in Scotland.

1911 census: the family were living at Brafferton. George was single and working as a cartwright on his own account.

Unit: unknown.

RICHARDSON, Joseph. b. 1892 at Sherburn Colliery, Co. Durham. Brother of George above.

Army number: 260701. Rank: Private. Unit: 500 Labour Corps.

RIPPETH, Joseph. b. 1899 in North Shields.

Parents: Thomas George Rippeth and Dora Jane Westall.

Family: one brother, four sisters. Married Grace Foster 1925.

Rank: Able Seaman.

Unit: Royal Navy, HMS Conqueror.

Joseph served from 1916 to 1922. He was based at Scapa Flow. He was in Russia 1917 in the Russian Revolution.

Joseph Rippeth is the father of Joseph Rippeth of Newton Aycliffe.

Photograph courtesy of Joseph Rippeth

RIPPETH, Robert Westall. b. 1898 in North Shields. Brother of Joseph above.

Rank: Able Seaman. Unit: Royal Navy. Based at North Shields.

Milli Tezcan-Fotooh, 8 GBV

Greenfield Community College, WW1 Boxes

Connor Radford, 8ROY

ROBINSON, Charles Edwin. b. 1896 in Brafferton.

Parents: William Marshall Robinson and Emily Florence Lovett.

Army number: 104149. Rank: Sapper. Unit: 227th Field Company, Royal Engineers.

Charles Edwin Robinson had attested June 23, 1915 at Thornaby on Tees. He was 19 years old and an apprentice joiner. Charles was tested and received a Proficiency Certificate which found him very good. September 8, 1915 Charles was at Marton Hall.

Charles was wounded in his right shoulder by a bullet and taken prisoner March 28, 1918 at Peronne. His last place of internment was Stralsund, Germany.

May 31, 1918 Charles' mother Emily sent a letter to the Royal Engineers at Chatham, enquiring as to whether she was entitled to her allowance which had been made by her son to her. June 14 Emily was asked to send the correspondence she had received from her son stating that he was a prisoner of war. Emily sent this June 17, asking for it to be returned to her when they had done with it. Charles' letter was forwarded to the Secretary of the Royal Engineers Prisoner of War Fund.

Charles was repatriated to Hull, arriving at the camp December 30, 1918. He departed the camp January 1, 1919. Charles was demobbed April 9, 1919.

Charles was one of the repatriated prisoners of war that were guests at the 'Welcome Home Dinner, Concert and Dance' given by the Darlington Committee for the Entertainment of Wounded Soldiers. This was held at the Temperance Hall, Darlington, May 7, 1919.

Wall depicting bombardment of church at Albert, France

ROBINSON, Percy. b. 1892 in Hartlepool.

Parents: John and Elizabeth Robinson of Hartlepool.

1901 census: Percy, his parents and brothers Harold, Arthur and John were living at 31, Tweed Street, West Hartlepool. John Robinson was a Marine Engine Driller.

1911 census: family were living at 43, Rokeby Street, West Hartlepool. Percy was an apprentice brass moulder.

Army number: 5498. Rank: Gunner. Unit: Durham Royal Garrison Artillery.

Percy joined the Durham Royal Garrison Artillery November, 6, 1911. Percy was entered as Robson and not Robinson, and this continued throughout his war career even though he signed forms as Percy Robinson.

Percy was 19 years 6 months old when he enlisted in 1911. He was 5' 8 ¼" tall, 10 stone, had good vision and his physical development was strong. Preliminary training was November 6, 1911 and annual training took place August 4, 1912 to August 18, 1912, August 2, 1913 to August 16, 1913 and August 2, 1914 to August 4, 1914 when he was enlisted for War Service.

Percy was embodied August 5, 1914. He served in France December 10, 1915 to October 12, 1916 and at home till April 4, 1917.

Percy returned to England for munitions service. R.H.C. Lyons, RAMC had certified that Percy was fit for any class of munition work September 5, 1916 and sent this to OC 41st Siege Battery, RGA. October 17, 1916 Percy was instructed to report immediately to the O/C No. 71, T.T. Depot, 42, Middlegate, Hartlepool to be taken on the supernumerary strength of that depot. Percy received a new number, 337603.

Percy was working at The Central Marine Engine Works, West Hartlepool from October 16, 1916 to March 21, 1917. April 4, 1917 Percy was discharged from service. His military character assessed as very good.

Percy received his 1914-1915 Star March 11, 1921.

Royal Garrison Artillery badges courtesy Bill Lowery

ROBINSON, William Lincoln. b. 1898 in Scorton, Yorkshire.

Parents: William and Mary Jane Robinson. William was a farmer at Fountain Head Farm in 1901.

1911 census: William was a widower living with his two children, William Lincoln and Agnes Jane, at Scorton, Yorkshire. William was now a carting contractor.

Attested: June 5, 1916 at Croft on Tees. William was 18 years 6 months old. He was 5' 7" tall and weighed 133 lbs. William was a gardener living at Kirkbank, Middleton Tyas.

Army number: 45364. Rank: Private.

Unit: 6th then 2nd Battalion, Yorkshire Regiment (Green Howards).

William joined the Green Howards December 27, 1916. He embarked at Folkestone March 25, 1917 and joined the 6th Battalion, Yorkshire Regiment at Etaples.

William was posted to the 2nd Battalion May 16, 1918. William worked as a Lewis Machine Gun operator. He was back in the U.K. January 11, 1919 and was discharged February 15, 1919.

William Lincoln Robinson is the great uncle of Annette Bowmer of Aycliffe.

Photograph courtesy of Annette Bowmer.

ROBINSON, William. b. 1894 in Aycliffe.

Attested: August 28, 1914 at Darlington.

Army number: 90277. Rank: Gunner. Unit: 105 Battery, Royal Field Artillery.

William was 19 years 262 days old and working as a labourer when he attested.

William joined the 105 Battery October 1, 1914.

William was living in Heighington Street August 20, 1920 when he received his 1914-1915 Star and British War Medal and his Victory Medal in 1921.

ROBINSON, William. b. in Ricknall, near Aycliffe, Co. Durham. William was baptized May 26, 1895 in St. Andrew's Church, Aycliffe.

William's parents were John Thomas and Jane Ann Robinson of Monks End, Aycliffe. John was a platelayer. William had 3 sisters: Emily, Cissie and Gladys.

Attested: January 7, 1915 at Darlington.

Army number: 3/4042326. Rank: Driver. Unit: Army Service Corps.

William was 19 years, 9 months old, and was 5' 6 ¾" tall. January 22, 1915 William passed his test in butchery at Aldershot and was assessed as fair.

William joined the 288 Company, 37 Division Trans. in France.

ROBSON, James Edward. b. 1886 in Heighington.

Parents: William Robson, born South Church.

1891 census: William Robson, a widower, and his four sons, Lewis, John Percy, James Edward and Frank M, his daughter Caroline M, his sister Alice Robson, and nephew Thomas J Brown, were living at Hambleton Farm, Coatham Mundeville.

1901 census: James Edward is entered as Edward.

Army number: 3277. Rank: Private. Unit: Remount Corps of the Army Service Corps.

Attested: October 7, 1914 at Bishop Auckland. He was 28 years 11 months old, 5' 5 ¼" tall and weighed 142 lbs. He had brown eyes and hair and had a fresh complexion. His occupation was groom.

James Edward joined the Expeditionary Force in France October 19, 1914. He was home from June 18, 1916 to September 17, 1916. James Edward had fallen May 5, 1916 and sprained his ankle near Sargueux and was at Rouen for one month. His ankle was put in plaster of Paris June 22, 1916 and the plaster was still on July 3. He was then transferred to Gartshore Hospital and later discharged from Springburn Woodside Hospital August 8, 1916.

James Edward was on leave October 21 to November 1, 1917, and then October 22 to December 6, 1918.

Medals: 1914 Star, Victory Medal, and the British War Medal.

<u>WWI Poem</u>

Dead and injured

Scattered all around

The worst place a man can be

Here in this God forsaken place

I must be careful in this Earthly Hell

Hearing my fallen comrades

Feeling helpless as their cries echo across the battlefield

The smell of burning flesh and gunpowder

Leaving a foul taste in my throat

Will there be no escape from this Nightmare

Joshua M, aged 10

Aycliffe Village Primary School

ROWELL, Robert. b. 1898 in New Seaham, Co. Durham.

Parents: Thomas Rowell and Margaret Ann Heppell.

Robert had 3 siblings in the 1911 census. The family lived at 2, California Street, New Seaham.

Unit: Unknown.

Robert Rowell was gassed during the war. He died 1922, age 23.

Robert is the uncle of Norma Cummings of Aycliffe.

David Hugill, 8ROY

Greenfield Community College, WW1 Boxes

Jamie Smedley, 8GBV

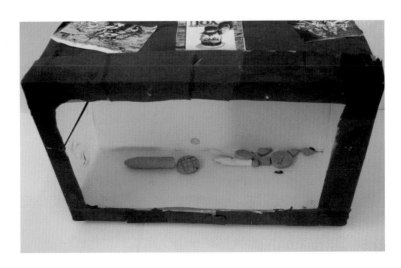

SARGEANT, Arthur Huntly.

b. 1899 in Northampton.

Family: son of Henry and Harriet Elizabeth Sargeant.

The family were originally shoemakers from Northampton but moved to Esh Winning, where they worked as coal miners.

1911 census: family living at 23, South Terrace, Esh Winning. Later they moved to Hollinside, near Lanchester. Arthur was 12 and still at school.

Army number: 30706. Rank: Private.

Unit: 7th Battalion, Lincolnshire Regiment.

Killed in Action: August 8, 1917.

Buried: Brown's Copse Cemetery, Roeux, near Arras. Grave Reference: IV. A.50.

SARGEANT, John (Jack). b. 1892 in Northampton. Brother of Arthur above.

Army number: 1379. Rank: Private. Unit: 8th Battalion, Durham Light Infantry.

Attested: March 15, 1910 to join the Territorial Army, age 18 years 3 months old. He was 5' 3" tall, his chest was 33" and he had good vision. Jack had done annual training at Rothbury, July, 1910, Strensall, July, 1911, Scarborough, July 1912 and 1913.

Jack re-engaged March 14, 1914. He was now 22 years old. He was embodied August 5, 1914 to April 18, 1915. Jack was then sent abroad April 19, 1915. One week later, April 26, 1915, Jack was killed in action near Ypres, Belgium. His name is on the Menin Gate, Panel 36 and 38.

April 17, 1920, his father Henry Sargeant acknowledged receiving Jack's 1914-1915 Star, November 26, 1920 his British War Medal and May 20, 1921 Jack's Victory Medal.

Arthur Huntly Sargeant and Jack Sargeant are the great uncles of Vivien Ellis of Newton Aycliffe.

Photographs courtesy Vivien Ellis

124

SCOTT, Walter Robert. b. 1881 in Aycliffe.

Parents: Peter Cockburn and Margaret Scott, both of Scotland. Peter owned the saw mill at Monks End, Aycliffe. He was a builder and joiner.

1911 census: Walter had been married for 3 years and had one daughter, Elsie, age 1. He was a master joiner, living in Aycliffe. There was a visitor, Edith Lane, age 20, presumably his wife's sister, as he had married Sarah Jane Lane, November 26, 1907. He had a son, Walter Frederick Scott, born January 20, 1914.

Walter was the uncle of William Scott, who was killed in 1918.

Army number: 4901. Rank: Private. Unit: 3/244 Durham Light Infantry, 5 Reserve.

Attested: December 10, 1915. He was mobilized July 4, 1916 and posted September 1, 1916. Walter was 34 years, 10 months old, and was 5' 6 ¾" tall. He lived at Skerne House, (the Saw Mill), Aycliffe.

November 4, 1916 he embarked at Folkestone and landed at Boulogne. He was posted to 9th Battalion, Durham Light Infantry and then from that he was posted February 3, 1917 to the Road Construction Unit at Abbeville.

Walter was transferred and posted to the 3/4 Road Construction Company August 8, 1917 as a Pioneer, WR/30795.

Walter had holiday leave December 18, 1918. March 1919 he signed that he was not suffering from any disability at Saint-Symphorien. He was 38 years old.

Walter received his British War Medal and Victory Medal June 12, 1922.

SCOTT, Henry. b. 1884 in Shildon.

Parents: John and Ellen Scott from Arkengarthdale in Yorkshire.

1901 census: family were living at Orlands, Aycliffe. John Scott died before the 1911 census. His widow Ellen and son Harry (Henry) are both entered as Coal Dealer, living at Orleans, Aycliffe.

Army number: 4816/4. Rank: Private. Unit: 2/4th Royal Scots.

Attested: December 11, 1915 at Newcastle upon Tyne. Harry was 32 years old. He was 5' 5" tall, 140 lbs and had good physical development. He had blue eyes and grey hair.

His medical judged him only fit for home service due to sight impediment. He was posted May 11, 1916.

By August 29, 1916 Harry was recommended for discharge as he suffered vertigo from an injury to the head prior to embodiment and this came into effect September 6, 1916.

Greenfield Community College, WW1 Boxes

SEARLE, Alick. b. 1895 in Aycliffe.

Parents: John Searle and Sarah Hadrick.

Family: brothers John, Henry, sister Annie.

1901 census: the family were living at North Terrace, Aycliffe. Alick's grandmother, Mary Hadrick, age 82, a widow, was living with the family.

Army number: 39868. Rank: Corporal. Unit: 21st Durham Light Infantry, then 13th York and Lancaster Regiment.

Attested: November 13, 1915 at Darlington, age 20 years, 10 months. Alick was a shop assistant. He was 5' 6" tall and named his sister, Miss A Searle, as next of kin.

Posted November 16, 1915. He was appointed Lance Corporal, unpaid, October 12, 1916. He was transferred to BEF December 18, 1916 and posted January 15, 1917. He was appointed Corporal and posted August 19, 1918.

Alick received his Protection Certificate March 8, 1919 and had signed that he was not claiming for a disability February 26, 1919.

Pte. Harry Searle, Northumberland Fus., brother of Miss Searle, Durham-rd., Aycliffe.

SEARLE, Harry (Henry William). b. 1883 in Aycliffe.

Brother of Alick above.

Army number: 1149. Rank: Private.

Unit: 17th Battalion, Northumberland Fusiliers.

1911 census: Henry is 27, single, and working as a railway clerk. He was a boarder at 3, Alexandra Road, Morpeth.

Newspaper cutting from the scrapbook of

Mrs Ida Hadrick

SEARLE, John. b. 1891 in Aycliffe. Brother of Alick and Harry above.

Army number: 286702. Rank: Gunner. Unit: 2 Battery, Royal Garrison Artillery.

SEARLE, Robert. b. 1900 at Ricknall Mill Farm.

Parents: Thomas and Mary Searle of Ricknall Mill, Preston le Skerne.

1901 census: there was a brother William, age 5, and a cousin, Thomas Searle, age 9, at the mill.

1911 census: there was also a sister Lucy, age 8.

Unit: unknown.

Matthew Venus, 8GBV

Greenfield Community College, WW1 Boxes

Lucy Cumming, 8GBV

SHELMERDINE, James, M.M. b. January 21, 1890 in Ashton under Lyne, Lancashire.

Parents: James Shelmerdine and Sarah Burrows.

1911 census: James junior worked at the Ashton Corporation Electricity Works.

Army number: 351762. Rank: Private.

Unit: 9th Battalion, Manchester Regiment.

Attested: May 2, 1915.

Family: wife Mary Elizabeth Dean. Mary was the daughter of John Herbert Dean, and Charlotte Alice Hyde of 16, Ashlynne, Ashton under Lyne.

James and Mary were married in the Parish Church of Ashton under Lyne June 12, 1915.

Photograph courtesy Vivien Ellis

AWARDED MILITARY MEDAL

Electricity Works Employe who Joined the Ashton Territorials

Private James Shelmerdine, Ashton Territorials, has written to his wife at 16 Ashlynne, Ashton, stating that he has been awarded the Military

Saturday, March 23, 1918 The Reporter newspaper of Ashton under Lyne had a photograph and article about James Shelmerdine. He had written to Mary to tell her that he had been awarded the Military Medal and that he was sending her a copy of the orders containing the information.

James first went to France March 26, 1916. He went again and had been in France for the last twelve months from the date of the article.

By the time the article appeared in the newspaper on the 23rd March, James sadly had been dead for two days.

James was killed at Pozières, March 21, 1918.

James is commemorated on the Pozières Memorial,

Panel 64 - 67.

Private JAMES SHELMERDINE.

Medal, and he sends a copy of the orders containing the information. Private Shelmerdine, who was formerly employed at the Ashton Corporation Electricity Works, joined the army on May 2nd, 1915, and went abroad on March 26th, 1916. He has been in France for the last twelve months.

James Shelmerdine's medals

by kind permission of the Trustees of the Museum of the Manchester Regiment

James' wife, Mary Dean, was the great aunt of Vivien Ellis of Newton Aycliffe.

SMITH, Albert. b. October 10, 1891 in St. Luke's, Finsbury, London.

Parents: John and Catherine Smith, who owned a fish shop. In the 1911 census they were living at 53, Bath Street, St. Luke's.

Army number: 61012. Rank: Sergeant.

Unit: 66th Battery, Royal Field Artillery.

Attested: January 24, 1910. Albert was 19 years and 3 months old. He enlisted for 6 years. He was 5' 7" tall, had a sallow complexion, brown eyes and dark brown hair. He had tattoos on his left forearm.

The battery armed with six 18 pounder field guns became part of the Divisional Artillery of the 7th Meerut Division of the 3rd (Lahore) Corps of the Indian Army. A Regular Division of the Indian Army it arrived in France in October 1914.

December 1915 the Division was directed to Mesopotamia where it remained until December 1917 when it was posted to Egypt.

The Division also served in Palestine.

On discharge January 23, 1922 Albert had served 9 years 147 days, 2 years 218 days of which were served in the reserve. His character was described as very good, honest, sober and trustworthy.

Albert served as an ARP warden in WW2. Albert is the father of Mrs Lilian Wheeler and grandfather of Christopher Wheeler of Aycliffe.

Photographs and information courtesy of Christopher Wheeler

SMITH, Edward. b. 1898 in Consett, Co. Durham.

Parents: Charles Smith, born North Shields, Northumberland, and Esther, born Jarrow, Co. Durham.

Edward had 4 sisters. In the 1911 census the family was living at 7, Berryedge Road, Consett.

1914 Edward was an apprentice fitter and turner in the locomotive and steam crane repair shop of the Consett Iron Company.

Towards the end of August 1914, Edward joined up. He had gone to Newcastle and told the local recruiting sergeant that he was 18. The sergeant told him "You are a fine big chap, you had better say you are 19", which Edward did. Edward joined the Northumberland Fusiliers. They paraded on the Town Moor under volunteer corporals and sergeants, one of whom told them "Aroond aboot turn".

Edward trained for 10 days, sleeping in railway carriages. Edward's father had threatened to tell the authorities his real age, but Edward said he would go elsewhere if he did and would not tell him where he was.

Winston Churchill, First Lord of the Admiralty, had formed a Naval Brigade formed by Anson, Howe, Hood and Nelson. The pay was 1/3d a day instead of the 1/- a day for the army. Volunteers were asked for and Edward joined up to the Anson division.

Churchill took over Crystal Palace and called it HMS Victory. Edward trained there for 3 months and was then sent to Blandford Downs in Dorset. Edward was given an army khaki uniform, the only difference being a khaki sailor's cap with a ribbon with the name of the battalion.

After 3 months they entrained at Avonmouth to join the troopship Grandtully. Edward landed at Port Said on his 17th birthday. After 10 days they went by train to Alexandria, and boarded the S.S. Caledonia, joining the 1st Lancashires, Dublins, Munsters and Enniskillens and they sailed to Gallipoli.

April 25, 1915, before 5 a.m., a steam pinnace and 5 cutters took the troops ashore. There were a few casualties, but the 1st Lancashires, further east on W beach, suffered, losing 90 men on the strong barbed wire.

May 6th Edward was advancing in 50 yard rushes when his foot was shot by a machine gun bullet. Edward was taken by stretcher bearers back to camp. He was then sent to Malta, where he had 2 operations. He caught Maltese fever which nearly killed him. Edward was returned to Portland Naval Hospital. After another operation on his foot he was declared fit for service. However, while training or marching his foot kept swelling up and so he was returned to hospital.

Edward was discharged February 26, 1916 and returned back home to Consett, where he resumed his apprenticeship, making up for lost time by doing overtime. He finished his apprenticeship when he was 21.

Edward eventually emigrated to New Zealand, and worked as an engineer at Dunedin Hospital. He retired age 64 in 1962 when his injured foot caused him problems.

Edward is the uncle of Marie Holden of Aycliffe who supplied the photograph and information.

STEVENSON, G.

This photograph of G. Stevenson was found in The Northern Star for October 18, 1916.

Private G. Stevenson, Aycliffe
(died of wounds).

STOCKS, George. b. 1880 in Northowram, Yorkshire.

Parents: Michael and Ellen Stocks. He had six siblings in the 1891 census. George married Edith Brooks Tingle November 12, 1910 at Birstall, Yorkshire.

1911 census: George was working as a teamster.

Army number: 84451. Rank: Driver. Unit: Royal Regiment of Artillery (R.A. & R.F.A).

Attested: January 26, 1915 at Pontefract. He was 33 years 3 months old, residing at Belton Street, Streethouse, near Wakefield.

George was posted to the 21 Reserve Battery, R.F.A. in France June 26, 1915. George had leave in the U.K. September 22, 1918 to October 6, 1918.

George Stocks is the great grandfather of Anne Brown of Aycliffe.

STOREY, William. b. 1888 in Consett, Co. Durham.

Parents: Robert and Elizabeth Storey.

1911 census: family at 6, Edward Street, Consett. William was 23 and working as a labourer at the steelworks.

William married Amy Williamson in 1913.

Army number: 21151. Rank: Corporal. Unit: 13th Battalion, Durham Light Infantry.

William died April 6, 1916. William is commemorated at Bully-Grenay Communal Cemetery, French Extension.

William Storey was the brother of Edmund Leadbitter's grandmother.

Herbert Thomas on his daughter Vera's wedding day

THOMAS, Herbert. b. 1898 in Hurworth, Co. Durham.

Parents: Robert and Isabel Thomas.

Wife: Georgina Webb.

1911 census: Robert was a blacksmith with 7 children.

Army number: 39367, then 4435695.

Rank: Corporal.

Unit: D Company, 1st Battalion, Durham Light Infantry.

Herbert Thomas served in India during WW1.

September 18, 1917 Herbert was at Cherat.

December 15, 1917 Herbert was at Rawal Pindi, Punjab.

After the war Herbert was sent to Germany as part of the occupation forces. In 1921 he worked in the Officers Mess at Koln, Germany.

Herbert Thomas is the father of Vera Brunton of Aycliffe. Photograph courtesy Vera Brunton.

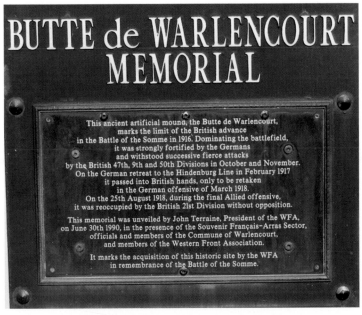

Butte de Warlencourt Memorial, Somme

THOMPSON, Wilfred. b. 1898 in Eldon, Co. Durham.

Parents: John William and Mary Thompson.

1911 census: family living at 74, West Chilton Terrace, Chilton.

Army number: 3/30574. Rank: Private. Unit: 3rd and 2nd Lincolnshire Regiment.

Attested: November 6, 1916. He was a labourer at a forge and was living at Tannery Cottages, Travellers Rest, Aycliffe. Wilfred was 18 years and 10 months old. He was 5' 1 ½". His next of kin was his father, John William Thompson.

March 1, 1917 Wilfred embarked at Folkestone and disembarked the same day at Boulogne. The next day he joined the Postal 8th Battalion at Calais.

March 21, 1917 Wilfred was in the field. He received a gunshot wound to his right leg April 18, 1917 and was sent on the Princess Elizabeth back to England. Wilfred was given furlough. His regiment now the 8th Lincolnshire.

By January 8, 1918 Wilfred was back in France. June 1, 1918 he was wounded in action. His father sent a letter July 1, 1918 enquiring after his son as he had heard he was in hospital. Wilfred was wounded again September 21. He was given furlough again October 29, 1918 to November 4, 1918. His address was now Low Moor House, Simpasture, Aycliffe. He was considered fit for the Command Depot by R. Harkness at the Northern General Hospital.

Wilfred was transferred to the Reserve January 24, 1919 and received his Protection Certificate and advance of £2 and 28 days furlough .

Wilfred re-enlisted June 4, 1919 to the Royal Army Ordnance Corps for service with the North Russia Relief Corps and was allotted the army number S/9722.

THOMPSON, Thomas. Probably brother of Wilfred above as his address is Simpasture in the 1918 Absentee Voters' List.

Army number: 44738. Unit: Royal Garrison Artillery.

TIFFNEY, Edwin. b. 1897 at Kirk Deighton, Yorkshire.

Parents were John Thomas and Eliza Tiffney. John was a farm man.

1911 census: the family were at Patience Lane, Copt-Hewick, Ripon, Yorkshire. Edwin had 8 siblings, and was still at school.

Army number: 2920 then 201031. Rank: Private. Unit: West Yorkshire Regiment.

Edwin went to France October 14, 1915.

He died September 27, 1916, age 19, and is commemorated on the Thiepval Memorial, Pier and Face 2A. 2C and 2D.

Edwin is also commemorated on the Spa Gardens War Memorial in Ripon and on the Memorial Boards in Sharow Church, near Ripon.

Edwin is the great uncle of Diane Robinson of Newton Aycliffe.

TIMBS, Alfred. b. 1893 in Yapham, Yorkshire.

Parents: William and Harriet Timbs.

1911 census: Alfred's parents were living at Yapham, near Pocklington. They had been married 28 years and had had 17 children, 6 of whom had died.

Army number: 3423. Rank: Private. Unit: 5th Battalion, Yorkshire Regiment.

TIMBS, Arthur Thomas. b. 1887 in Yapham.

Army number: 81373. Rank: Gunner. Unit: Royal Field Artillery.

TIMBS, George Henry. b. 1888 in Yapham.

Army number: 28912. Rank: Private. Unit: Yorkshire Regiment.

TIMBS, Richard. b. 1897 in Yapham.

Army number: 3406. Rank: Private. Unit: 5th Battalion, Yorkshire Regiment.

Killed August 15, 1916. Commemorated: Bailleul Communal Cemetery, Nord, France.

Richard Timbs is the great uncle of Kate Baker of Aycliffe.

Serre Road No. 2 Cemetery, France

UNKNOWN

This photograph was among those Mrs Ida Hadrick allowed the Society to scan.

We suspect it may be a member of the Searle family. Any information would be appreciated.

Shell craters at Beaumont-Hamel

WAKE, Thomas Henry. b. 1890 in Bamburgh, Northumberland.

Bamburgh Brothers Killed.

Private Wilfred Hereward Wake.   Private Thomas Henry Wake.

Parents: Richard and Mary Wake. Richard Wake was the lodgekeeper of Bamburgh Castle.

Army number: 1989.

Rank: Private.
Unit: C Coy 7th Battalion, Northumberland Fusiliers.

Enlisted at Alnwick.

His younger brother, **Wilfred Hereward Wake,** b. 1895, Private 1598, was already a member of the same Territorial Force and had been called up immediately to join his regiment.

After training for several months both brothers were sent to the Front. After two days both brothers were killed near Ypres April 26, 1915. Both are commemorated on the Menin Gate.

Thomas was 25 and had been a painter, employed by Mr R. W. Mackenzie, Seahouses.

Wilfred was 20 and worked as a tailor employed by Messrs. R. Coxon and Sons, Seahouses.

According to the newspaper article about them, both were fond of sport, cricket and football. Thomas (Tommy) was well known in the North Northumberland Football League, which he represented in international matches.

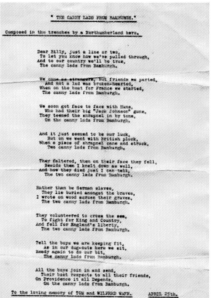

A poem, "The Canny Lads from Bamburgh" was written about them, composed in the trenches by a Northumberland hero.

This poem, and one composed by their father Richard Wake, are shown left and right.

Thomas and Wilfred are great uncles of Sandra Willoughby of Newton Aycliffe, who supplied the photographs and poems.

WALKER, Jacob. b. 1878 in Aycliffe.

Parents: William and Margaret Walker of Aycliffe.

1881 census: they were living next door to the Royal Telegraph in Aycliffe.

1891 census: family in King Street, Darlington.

1901 census: Jacob Walker was still single, age 23 and worked as a bricklayer.

Jacob married a Mary (Dale?) in 1910.

1911 census: living in Railway Cottages, Haswell, working as a platelayer for the railways.

Army number: M2/188815. Rank: Private. Unit: Army Service Corps.

Medals: Victory and British medals.

WALKER, Jacob.

Rank: Sapper. Unit: Royal Engineers.

Jacob Walker was one of the repatriated prisoners of war that were guests at the *'Welcome Home Dinner, Concert and Dance'* given by the Darlington Committee for the Entertainment of Wounded Soldiers. This was held at the Temperance Hall, Darlington, May 7, 1919.

Jacob Walker lived at the Orlands, Aycliffe.

WALKER, Harry. b. 1890 in Aycliffe.

Parents: William and Jane Walker of High Copelaw, Woodham. William Walker was a farmer and had had nine children.

1911 census: Harry was 21, single, working on his father's farm.

Army number: 108441. Rank: Sapper. Unit: Royal Engineers.

Attested: August 5, 1915. Harry was 26 years 5 months old. He was a carpenter and was willing to serve as a carpenter in the Royal Engineers. Harry was 5' 9 ½" tall and his next of kin was his father William. Harry had taken a trade proficiency test July 27, 1915.

January 21, 1916, he embarked at Devonport, destination Alexandria. Three months later, April 13, 1916, he embarked at Alexandria and disembarked 8 days later at Marseilles.

Harry had 10 days leave to July 31, 1917 and leave January 20 to February 9, 1918, and 12 days leave to December 19, 1918. Harry was despatched to the UK January 31, 1919 and received his Protection Certificate February 4, 1919.

WALLIS, John George. b. 1884 in Stockton on Tees, Co. Durham.

Parents: George and Jane Wallis.

1901 census: George Wallis, 43, Coachman, born Marton, Yorkshire, and his wife Jane, 35, born Bishopton, Durham, were living at Halnaby, near Croft, Yorkshire. Their son, John G Wallis was 16, a Joiner's Apprentice.

Family: married Ann Ethel Turnbull 1909. Ann was born 1885 in Heighington.

1911 census: married for 1 year and had a 3 month old daughter, Jane, born in Coundon. They lived at 3, Frederick Street, Coundon in 1911. John George Wallis was a joiner and cartwright. They had 3 more children: Alice, born 1914, John George, born 1917, and Thomas, born 1920.

Army number: 146166. Rank: Private. Unit: 3/3 SARB, Royal Garrison Artillery.

Attested: Thursday, May 4, 1915, at Ferryhill. He was 31 years and 3 months old and was now living at Woodham Cottages, Rushyford. He sat a trade proficiency test. He passed this test and a telegram was sent from the Central Recruiting Office at Leeds to the Ferryhill Recruiting Officer informing them of this and that John had been ordered to report to the office at Ferryhill to complete documents and be there ready to go away on Monday. John received his telegram the same day telling him to report on Friday, May 5 to his recruiting officer.

There is a headed letter from John's employer, Davidson & Sons, (Motor Cars, horses, brakes and Conveyance) at West House, Coundon, who was agreeable to his release.

Pozières Memorial, France

WATERWORTH, Thomas. b.1897 in Ashton in Makerfield, Lancashire.

Parents: John and Jane Waterworth.

1911 census: the family were living at 41, Post Office Street, Low Spennymoor, Co. Durham. His father was a coal miner hewer and Thomas was a pit bank belt lad.

Attested: October 3, 1914. He was 18 years 1 month old.

Army number: 2994, then 250306. Rank: Sergeant. Unit: 6th Battalion, Durham Light Infantry.

Thomas served in France from August 20, 1915 until January 1, 1919, and was discharged January 30, 1919.

Thomas Waterworth is the brother of Alice Ann Waterworth, wife of Thomas Lowery of Byers Green.

Thomas and Alice Lowery are the grandparents of Bill Lowery of Newton Aycliffe.

Durham Light Infantry badges courtesy Bill Lowery

WATSON, Joseph. b. 1898 in Hull, Yorkshire.

Parents: Joseph Watson, born Gateshead, and Alice Robinson, born Aycliffe.

1911 census: living in Aycliffe. Joseph Watson senior was 52 and worked as a colliery labourer. Joseph Watson junior was 13 years old and at school.

Army number: 20529. Rank: Private. Unit: 13th Company, Coldstream Guards.

Attested: November 27, 1916, at West Hartlepool. He was 18 years old and worked as a railway goods clerk for N.E.R. Joseph was 5' 8" tall, weighed 140 lbs, and had brown eyes and dark brown hair.

Joseph was admitted to hospital December 16, 1916, suffering from syncope. Joseph had told the doctors that he had had a bad attack of pneumonia at the age of 4 years and had suffered from heart trouble since. He had giddiness and fainting fits and shortness of breath. Joseph had only managed 3 days work since enlisting. The doctors found that he was suffering from valvular disease of the heart.

Joseph was discharged as he was no longer physically fit for war service. His character was described as sober and hardworking.

WHEADON, Charles. b. 1882 in Darlington.

Parents: William and Elizabeth Ann Wheadon.

Family: Charles married Mary Teresa Sowerby in 1901 at Darlington.

1911 census: living at 3, Leonard Street, Bank Top, Darlington. They had had 6 children, 2 of whom had died. Mary Teresa died in 1917.

Army number: 58573. Rank: Private. Unit: Machine Gun Corps.

Attested: December 11, 1915.

Charles lost a leg in the war and was discharged September 10, 1919.

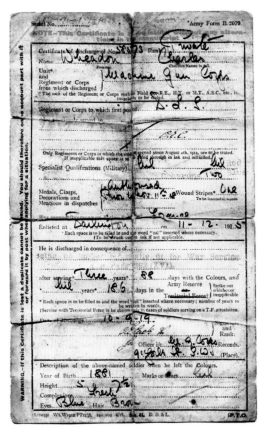

Charles married May Newsome in 1919 in Darlington. They lived at 4, The Orlands, Aycliffe.

Charles is the grandfather of Peter Wheadon of Newton Aycliffe.

Charles' Discharge Certificate right, courtesy of Peter Wheadon

WHITE, James Walter. b. 1893 in Stillington.

Parents: James White, born Fishburn, railway platelayer for N.E.R. and Hannah M.

Family: three brothers and sisters.

1901 and 1911 censuses: family were living at Clarence Cottage, Simpasture.

Unit: unknown.

WHITE, Walter Donkin. b. June 8, 1890 in Hartlepool, Co. Durham.

Parents: William and Hannah White. William was a sailor.

1901 census: Walter was the 6th of 9 children.

Walter married Mary Zillah Johnson in 1914 in Hartlepool.

Service number: 909261. Unit: Merchant Navy.

Walter died at sea July 6, 1947. He was a Chief Steward with 30 years service.

Walter Donkin White is the grandfather of Thomas Hodgson of Aycliffe.

6

GREAT AYCLIFFE PARISH COUNCIL.

CHAIRMAN:
Mr. Christopher Kent.

CLERK:
MR. FRED RICHARDSON.

Aycliffe,
Darlington,
30th Jany. 1915.

Dear Sir,
I am in receipt of your letter
and pamphlet. re encouraging recruiting
which has been sounded in this Village.
The percentage is as follows. :—
Out of a population of 750.
34 have joined the Army, and a
further 10 men volunteered but failed
to pass the medical examination.

Thanking you in Anticipation
Yours very truly.
Fred Richardson

The Editor.
Weekly Despatch.
Carmelite House.
London E.C

Reproduced by permission of Great Aycliffe Town Council and Durham County Records Office, Durham County Record Office CP/GA 15

WILSON, Maud Elizabeth. b. 1899.

Maud served as a nurse in France in World War 1, from 1914-1918.

She was awarded a medal for service in the front line, and her son, Eric White, still has this - a source of great pride for him. Eric still lives in Aycliffe.

WAAC Sgts Mess

Maud married Ernest White and ran the County Hotel in Aycliffe. She also delivered babies in Aycliffe.

Maud died August 1, 1970, age 71 and is buried in St. Andrew's Churchyard, Aycliffe.

WILSON, Robert Sharpe. b. June 27, 1900 in Coatbridge, Scotland.

Rank: Sergeant. Unit: Cameron Highlanders.

Robert first lived at Norton and then Heighington Street, Aycliffe.

Robert married the widowed Mena Waller, née McCormack, in 1938.

Robert is the step-grandfather of Wendy Etheridge of Aycliffe. Wendy kindly supplied the photograph and information.

GREAT AYCLIFFE PARISH COUNCIL.

CHAIRMAN:
Mr. C. Kent.

CLERK:
MR. FRED RICHARDSON.

Aycliffe,
Darlington,
20th February 1915.

"National Relief Fund"

Dear Sir,

Yours of the 9th inst: to hand re the above, which was placed before my Council on the 18th inst: when I was directed to say that, the Vicar of the Parish is making collections monthly for the various funds you include on your record sheet, there are also about one dozen Belgian refugees quartered at Coatham Hall, Coatham Mundeville, a village one mile from here, and the inhabitants of Aycliffe are helping in the need. but there is a Special Committee appointed to direct the course of the proceeds collected towards same. The above Council are collecting nothing towards the Fund as the district is only a working class one and men are having to much retained from their weekly wages towards theeyors funds etc.

The National Relief Fund
York House.
St James Palace. S.W.

Faithfully Yours
Fred Richardson

Reproduced by permission of Great Aycliffe Town Council and Durham County Records Office, Durham County Record Office CP/GA 15

WOOFF, Thomas William. b. 1899 in Skipton, Yorkshire.

Army number: 22549. Rank: Private.

Unit: 3rd Battalion, West Riding Regiment.

Thomas attested April 4, 1917 at Halifax. Thomas was 18 years 13 days old. He was 5' 9" tall, weighed 143 lbs, and his chest measurement was 36 ½".

He joined the 8th Training Reserve Battalion and then the 3rd Battalion, West Riding Regiment. Thomas was a waggoner.

January 31, 1918, Thomas was sent to France and then back home October 18, 1918 - he had been wounded October 12, 1918.

On Thomas's Dispersal Certificate of January 8, 1919, his address is 10, Rowland Street, Skipton. Thomas signed the receipt for his British War Medal January 9, 1921, and his Victory Medal March 16, 1921.

After being discharged from the army Thomas came to live in Aycliffe and lodged with Mary Burnside. Thomas later married Mary (née Smith) and worked as a logger.

Photographs courtesy of Roland Burnside

Thomas William Wooff is the step-grandfather of Roland Burnside of Aycliffe.

WRIGHT, Thomas. b. about 1891 in Gateshead, Co. Durham.

Parents: Thomas and Mary Wright.

Thomas married Harriet Batty in 1916 and later lived in Heighington.

From the photograph Thomas probably served in the Pioneer Battalion of the Royal Welch Fusiliers.

Thomas Wright is the great, great grandfather of Kian White of Aycliffe.

Photograph courtesy of Kian White

Life in the Trenches

Sharing everything

Parcels shared

Rats the size of cats bite your ear

And share your bed.

Armour shared

Injuries

Pain

Death

Is this sharing the price of war?

Kian White, aged 10

Aycliffe Village Primary School

YOUNG, James. b. October 12, 1889 in Diamond Terrace, West Auckland.

Mother: Catherine Young. No father is recorded on his birth certificate.

1891 and 1901 censuses: James lived with his grandmother, Margaret.

James married Mary Tray in 1910 and lived at 2 Maughan's Yard, Coundon, Co. Durham.

Army number: 2606. Rank: Private. Unit: 6th Battalion, Durham Light Infantry.

Attested: September 28, 1914.

James was 24 years of age and 5ft 4¼ inches tall with a 38" chest.

August 13, 1916 James embarked on a troop ship to Boulogne. August 18, 5 days after reaching France, James wrote his will leaving all of his possessions to his wife Mary Young.

He joined D Company, 14th Battalion, DLI September 14, 1916.

Sunday, September 24, at 8.00 a.m. enemy began shelling. The enemy attempted an attack on the DLI front but was driven back.

British heavy artillery opened fire but many shells fell short. One burst in the DLI trench and killed Oswald Alexander Herd and Private James Young, and wounded 2 others.

Oswald Alexander Herd is buried in the Guard's Cemetery, Lesboeufs.

James has no known grave and is commemorated on the Thiepval memorial, Pier and Face 14 A and 15 C.

James is also commemorated on the War Memorial near to Coundon Church.

James Young is the great uncle of Len Skelton of Newton Aycliffe.

Absent Voters' List.

PARLIAMENTARY COUNTY OF DURHAM.
SEDGEFIELD DIVISION.

AYCLIFFE POLLING DISTRICT A.

1 No.	2 Names in Full. (Surname first).	3 Qualifying Premises.	4 Description of Service, Ship, Regiment, Number, Rank, Rating, &c., or recorded address.	5 No.
		Parish of Brafferton.		
1	Firby, Ambrose Binks	Brafferton Mill	36095, 4th K.O.Y.L.I.	1
2	Tweddle, George	Brafferton	500838, 407 Agric. Coy. Labour Corps.	2
3	Robinson, Charles Edwin	Brafferton	104149, Royal Engineers	3
4	Robinson, Arthur	Brafferton	91348, Durham Light Infantry	4
		Parish of Coatham Munderville.		
5	Errington, John	Coatham Mundeville	M2/226153, 20th Aux. Petrol Co.	5
6	Biglin, Edward Wilfred	Whiley Hill	149211, 34th Army Brigade, R.F.A.	6
7	Biglin, Harry Watson William	Whiley Hill	83647, North. Fus.	7
8	Graham, James William	Coatham Mill	812, Pte. R.G.A.	8
9	Graham, Walter	Coatham Mill	242788, 10th West Yorks.	9
10	Marquis, David Cecil	Dean Head Farm	143310, Pte. A.S.C.	10
11	Richardson, William	Coatham Mundeville	41163, 2nd Royal Dublin Fusiliers	11
12	Robson, James Edward	Humbleton Farm	4th Remount Depot, A.S.C.	12
13	Scott, William	Coatham Mundeville		13
		Parish of Great Aycliffe		
14	Bainbridge, George	Well House	243308 Pte., 8 Yorks.	14
15	Bartram, Clarence	Clarence Farm	37366 Pte., 18 D.L.I.	15
16	Bayles, Tom	Bank Villa	2452 Lce.-Cpl. M.M.P.	16
17	Bellwood, John Alfred	The Wynd	283394 Sapper, 34 L.R.O.C. R.E.	17
18	Bland, Thomas Wm.	Sagar Hill	40119 Pte., 4 E. Yorks.	18
19	Blenkinsopp, Joseph	High Street	90189 Bomd., 51 R.F.A.	19
20	Boddington, Thomas	Travellers' Rest Inn	419002 Pte., 47 Lab. Co. West Yorks.	20
21	Boddy, Joseph	County Hotel	67365 Pte., 162 R.D.C.	21
22	Coulson, James Hutchinson	High Street	168751 Cpl., 487 Agr. Lab. Cps.	22
23	Crusher, Joseph Henry	Field House	127306 Bomd., 43 R.G.A.	23
24	Crusher, Thomas	Field House	521268 Pte., 412 Agr. Cor.	24
25	Crusher, Robert Barker	Field House	163149 Pte., 4th Div. R.E.	25
26	Dale, Robert Addison	Aycliffe House	277283 Private, 22nd D.L.I.	26
27	Denham, Matthew	West Terrace	202611 Private, 8 D.L.I.	27
28	Dent, Frederick	Murton House Farm	83785 Private, N.F.	28
29	Dickinson, David	Station Terrace	34672 Pte., 18 Beds., T.W.	29
30	Eade, Charles	The Vicarage	Lieut., 9 Mach. Gun Sect.	30
31	Ellwood, John Thomas	Heighington Street	33229 Pte., Trans. Sec. D.L.I.	31
32	Everson, Frederick	Tanyard Cottages	306188 Gunner, R.E. Tank Cps.	32
33	Farrell, Michael	Waterside	207045, 2 O. Yorks. L.I.	33
34	Firby, Ambrose	Holm Hill	306005, K.O.Y.L.I.	34
35	Garnsby, Rueben Clarence	North Row	6031 Co., 2 M.S., 14th N.F.	35
36	Garthwaite, Harry Mills	Chapel Square	46318 Sapper, 79 R.E.	36
37	Gell, Charles Frederick	North Row	27504 Sapper, 13 King's Lvrpl.	37

1

1	2	3	4	5
No.	Names in Full. (Surname first).	Qualifying Premises.	Description of Service, Ship, Regiment, Number, Rank, Rating, &c., or recorded address.	No.
38	Gill, Walter	Well House	96183 Pte., R.A.M.C.	38
39	Gladwin, Stephen Victor	Heighington Street	32943 Pte., 17 North. Fus.	39
40	Goodwin, Charles	Heighington Street	250501 Pte., 6 B. D.L.I.	40
41	Grey, John George	High Street	7271 Cpl., A/165 B. R. F.	41
42	Hadrick, Fred	High Row	13210 Pte., Bord. Reg.	42
43	Hall, John William	Heighington Street	450016 Pte., 17 Lab. Co. R.	43
44	Hall, Charles Ernest	Heighington Street	15981 Pte., 20 K.R., R.G.	44
45	Hanson, Jonathan	North Row	449720 Pte., 51 Lab. Bat.	45
46	Hewitt, John	Heighington Street	90206 Corp., R.F.A.	46
47	Hollingworth, Ernest	North Terrace	317255 Pte., R.E.	47
48	Jagger, George A.	North Row	201291 Driver, R.F.A.	48
49	Kendall, Robert	Heighington Street	301813, 14 B. Heavy Tank Corps	49
50	Kent, Harold Leslie	High Row	204390 Pte., 4 North. Fus.	50
51	Kent, Walter	High Street	596602 B Corp., 2 W. Yorks	51
52	Kent, Joseph Alfred	High Street	252695 A.M. R.A.F.	52
53	Kent, Joseph William	High Row	46319 Corp., 79 R.E.	53
54	Kent, George Edmund	High Row	46322 Sergt., 79 R.E	54
55	Kent, Cecil James	Diamond Villa	36563 Pte., 3 D.L.I.	55
56	Lambert, Charles Douglas	White Lodge	Captain, Ord. Mobile Workshop	56
57	Lockey, James	North Aycliffe	309287 Pte., R.E.	57
58	Lockey, George	North Aycliffe	911507 Pte., 46 Canadians	58
59	Lockey, Edwin Charles	North Aycliffe	312562 Pioneer, I.W. Docks, R.E.	59
60	Lockey, William	Marks End	39137 Pte., A.S.C.	60
61	Lowcock, Charles	Heighington Street	36666 Pte., 16 Yks. and Lancs.	61
62	Marshall, Moor	Heighington Station	2157 Pte., R.A.M.C.	62
63	Marshall, Gordon Osborne	Heighington Station	158314 Pte., R.F.C.	63
64	Marshall, Sydney	Heighington Station	34313 Pte., R.A.M.C.	64
65	Nelson, William	Heighington Station	46325 Pte., 9 Sig. Corps	65
66	Parker, James	Heighington Street	200558 Pte., 27 D.L.I.	66
67	Pearce, Robert Thomas	Marks' End	118504 Pte., 74 Bt. M.G.C	67
68	Plaskitt, Albert	Station Terrace	235248 Pte., 1/7 Midds.	68
69	Pratt, Edward	Orlands	202148 Pte., R.E.	69
70	Richardson, Joseph	East Row	260701 Pte., 500 Lab. Corps	70
71	Robinson, Thomas	North Terrace	46321 Sapper, 79 R.E.	71
72	Robinson, Joseph	High Row	203113 Pte., 5 D.L.I.	72
73	Robinson, Anthony	High Row	205923 Bomd. R.G.A.	73
74	Robinson, Arthur	North Row	734 Pte., 26 D.L.I.	74
75	Robinson, Frederick	North Row	7105 Pte., 9 D.L.I.	75
76	Robinson, Benjamin	North Row.	23022 Pte., 52 Notts and Derby	76
77	Robinson, George	Heighington Street	20108 Gunner, 14 Div. R.F.A.	77
78	Robinson, William	Heighington Street	90277 Driver, 64 Bt. R.F.A.	78
79	Robinson, William	Monks' End	3/4042326 37 Driv., A.S.C.	79
80	Sanderson, Thomas	Travellers' Rest	102630 Gunner, 143 R.G.A.	80
81	Scott, Charles Rutherford	North Terrace	46317 Lnce.-Cpl., 431 R.E.	81
82	Scott, Walter Robert	Skerne House	30795 Pte., 314 R.C. Coy., RE.	82
83	Searle, Henry William	North Terrace	1149, 17 North. Fus.	83
84	Searle, Alick	North Terrace	39768 Corp., 13 Yks. and Lncs.	84
85	Searle, John	North Terrace	286702 Gunner, 2 B., R.G.A.	85
86	Shaw, Robert	Monks' End	46323 Sapper, Cable Sect., R.E.	86
87	Stelling, Matthew	Monks' End	348636 Gunner, 315 R.G.A.	87
88	Thompson, Thomas	Simpasture	44738, R.G.A	88
89	Thompson, Wilfrid	Simpasture	30574, 2 Lincs.	89
90	Walker, Jacob	Orlands	Pte., R.E.	90
91	Walker, William	East Row	240331 Pte., 1/5 K.O.Y.L.I.	91
92	Watson, Ernest Percy Reginald	North Row	46320 Sapper, 5th Survey Corps. R.E.	92

2

List of regiments or services that those who served were a member of.

1. Alexandra, Princess of Wales Own Yorkshire Regiment

2. 32nd Battalion, Australian Infantry

3. Army Service Corps (M.T.)

4. Army Service Corps (H.T.) Company

5. Army Service Corps Mechanical Reserve Depot

6. Army Service Corps Remount Service

7. Border Regiment

8. Cameron Highlanders

9. Canadian Expeditionary Force

10. Coldstream guards

11. Durham Light Infantry

12. East Surrey Regiment

13. East Yorkshire Regiment

14. Essex Regiment

15. Forest of Dean Pioneers Gloucestershire Regiment

16. Gordon Highlanders

17. Green Howards (Yorkshire Regiment)

20. Highland Light Infantry

21. King's Own Liverpool Regiment

22. King's Own Royal Lancaster Regiment

23. King's Own Yorkshire Light Infantry

24. King's Royal Rifle Corps

25. Labour Corps

26. Lincolnshire Regiment

27. London Regiment, Queen Victoria Rifles

28. Machine Gun Corps

29. Manchester Regiment

30. Middlesex Regiment

31. New Zealand Rifle Brigade

32. Non Combatant Corps (Northern Company)

33. Northumberland Fusiliers

34. Nottingham and Derby Regiment, Sherwood Foresters

35. Royal Horse and Royal Field Artillery

36. Royal Army Medical Corps

37. Royal Army Service Corps Field Battery

38. Royal Engineers

39. Royal Field Artillery

40. Royal Flying Corps

41. Royal Fusiliers

42. Royal Garrison Artillery

43. Royal Navy

44. Royal Scot Fusiliers

45. Royal Welch Fusiliers

46. Seaforth Highlanders

47. South Lancashire Regiment

48. Tank Corps

49. York and Lancaster Regiment

50. Yorkshire Light Infantry

51. Yorkshire Regiment

52. West Yorkshire Regiment

Sources

Commonwealth War Graves Commission

The Northern Echo

The Evening Gazette

The Northern Star

The Darlington and Stockton Times

Original army documents in the possession of relatives of those who served

Information from the families of those who served

Information relevant to individuals who served taken from census details held by Ancestry.co.uk

"Annals of Aycliffe, A Parish of the Palatine" 1927 by Louisa Wilson

"Monumental Inscriptions, St. Andrew, Aycliffe, Co. Durham" by Cleveland Family History Society

"The Employees and Residents of Thornley, Ludworth & Wheatley Hill, their contribution in the Great War 1914-1918" by Wheatley Hill History Club

Aycliffe Parish Registers held at Darlington Library Local Studies Section

West Cemetery Darlington

Durham County Records Office, CP/GA 15, pages 6 & 7, and CC/C1 1/201